*pathways
to
happiness*

pathways
to
happiness

A DEVOTIONAL STUDY OF THE BEATITUDES

leonard griffith

ABINGDON PRESS   NEW YORK • NASHVILLE

PATHWAYS TO HAPPINESS

Copyright © 1964 by Abingdon Press

Library of Congress Catalog Card Number: 64-10601

SET UP, PRINTED, AND BOUND BY THE
PARTHENON PRESS, AT NASHVILLE,
TENNESSEE, UNITED STATES OF AMERICA

PATHWAYS TO HAPPINESS

preface /

I have always wanted to write a book on the Beatitudes, but have been deterred from doing so chiefly by the fear of repeating what others have written more adequately. The opening verses of the Sermon on the Mount are such familiar ground to students of the Bible that it scarcely seems possible to interpret them with new and compelling relevance. Yet it has so often been my experience that the freshest and most exciting insights break forth, not from the unexplored regions of Scripture, but from the well-trodden regions, the very passages that we have known and quoted

5

since childhood. Familiar as they may be to our minds, the Beatitudes never lose their fascination, simply because they challenge us to a way of life which has never been perfectly personified save by the One who enunciated them. Where, indeed, shall we find a man whose character measures up to *every* rule of the kingdom of God, and on whose tombstone the words of the fifth chapter of Matthew might be inscribed as representing the sum total of his life? Were there such a man, it could be said that he has discovered the secret of true happiness, for, as I have tried to emphasize in the following pages, the Beatitudes were originally offered to us as "pathways to happiness."

I submit this exposition of the Beatitudes with the prayer that it may illumine those paths along which we may walk with the happiest of men.

LEONARD GRIFFITH

contents/

contents

introduction/

HAVE WE A RIGHT TO HAPPINESS?

"The trouble with you Americans," said an Englishman, "is that you have to be so confoundedly happy. You have dedicated yourselves to the pursuit of happiness. You boast about it as an inalienable right, as though happiness were the supreme and absolute goal of all existence. Surely there are more important things in life than just being happy."

Let it be said that Americans have indeed asserted their right to the pursuit of happiness in the basic document of their national life, the Declaration of Independence. Thomas Jefferson, the brains behind this initial declaratory document, borrowed his ideas from the Englishman John Locke. Locke specified as the fundamental rights of man life, liberty, and property, but Jefferson considered the list inadequate. He made the significant change by which the word "happiness" was substituted for the word "property." Therefore we read that Americans, and presumably their British cousins, are endowed with certain inalienable rights—life, liberty, and the pursuit of happiness.

But does this represent the truth? Have we a right to happiness? The advertisers tell us that we have, and so do the vocal tranquilizers who mesmerize us with what they are pleased to call music on radio and television. Most people dream of happiness, plan for it, and live in a never-ending search for it. In the quest for happiness one man buys half a dozen homes; another goes into the wilderness. In the same search one woman becomes a nun; another, a harlot. Night clubs, race tracks, bingos, and marihuana all testify to a conviction in people that somewhere, somehow, there are deeds and diversions that can make them happy.

A middle-aged man sat in my vestry looking quite miserable, and as unyielding as the Rock of Gibraltar. I had called him in because I was the minister who had officiated at his wedding, baptized his three children, and counted him among the faithful members of my church. Now he had shocked all his friends by wrecking his own marriage and deserting his wife and children. He was having an affair with his secretary, but this, he assured me, was the result and not the cause of his estrangement from his wife. He found that he just didn't love his wife any more. He was no longer happy in his own home; and, since he was certain that every man has a right to be happy, presumably on any terms, he had now claimed this right, giving it priority over his obligations as a husband and a father.

Have we a right to happiness? If we turn to the Bible for an answer, our thoughts go immediately to the fifth chapter of Matthew, and especially to that familiar passage in the Sermon on the Mount known as the Beatitudes. Here is an entire discourse from the lips of Jesus with happiness as its theme. The verses begin, *"Blessed* are the poor in spirit. . . . *Blessed* are they that mourn. . . . *Blessed* are the meek. . . ."* Some modern translators frankly change the rendering of the Greek word *makarios* from "blessed" to "happy." To be sure, blessedness has a richer, larger, deeper, and more spiritual meaning than happiness, but blessedness contains happiness just as a red-hot iron contains fire. Indeed, this study of the Beatitudes has been entitled *Pathways to Happiness;* but before considering them individually, let us consider certain general truths that emerge from the Beatitudes and accept them as the biblical answer to the question, Have we a right to happiness?

The Christian life is essentially a happy life. That may sound like a trite statement, but we make it to correct the die-hard caricature of Christianity as a spiritual "wet blanket" that represses all normal impulses and smothers the spark of joy. The late C. S. Lewis told of a school child who was asked what he thought God was like. The child answered that, so far as he could make out, God is the kind of person who is

11

always snooping around to see if anyone is enjoying himself, so that he can put a stop to it. That describes, according to some of its critics and supporters, the role religion plays in life —the role of a Grand Inquisitor accompanied by a tune in a minor key.

Whoever entertains such an illusion will have difficulty deciding whether Jesus was a Christian; and it is certain that there are some ultrapious people who do harbor doubts on the matter. They approve the Christ of classical art, the "pale Galilean," the Man of Sorrows whose very presence makes innocent laughter and gaiety seem blasphemous. But what are they going to do with the winsome Jesus of the Gospels, the Man of Nazareth who took such delight in all the simple pleasures about him; who came eating and drinking, so that his enemies dubbed him a glutton and a winebibber; who enjoyed life's wholesome convivialities—a wedding, a banquet, a gathering of friends in the home; who mingled with publicans and sinners and attracted little children to his knee; who possessed such a sparkling sense of humor that flashed out in ludicrous word-pictures, like that of the man with a plank hanging out of his eye, painfully squinting as he removes a speck of sawdust from the eye of his brother? What will the religious bloodhounds do with that kind of Jesus, he who so obviously saw and shared man's longing to be happy; who wanted us to find happiness, and in the Beatitudes pointed a way?

Some religious leaders frankly despise the pursuit of happiness. Gautama Buddha counseled escape from life rather than enjoyment of it, and in this respect his teaching is diametrically opposite that of Christ. The Christian life is essentially a happy life; and if a man's Christianity does not elevate his spirit and give him in some measure the feeling of contentment which he craves, then it is not the religion of Jesus but a poor imitation. The kindest thing that can be said about an unhappy Christian is that he is suffering from a state of arrested spiritual development. It has been suggested that Christians are like apples. Even the finest apples in the early stages of growth are sour and green; only when the sun has done its perfect work do they become red and luscious. So human souls in the early stages of Christian experience are often green and sour, crabbed and full of acid. Subject them to the sun, however, the sunlight of Christ's radiant, exuberant personality, and all the juices of their nature will turn sweet and mellow, and they will find themselves at last in the kingdom of peace and joy.

The Beatitudes make it very plain that *happiness is a state of mind*. That must be so, else we can only accuse our Lord of talking arrant nonsense. "Let me tell you," he said, "who the blessed, the truly happy people are." And he enumerated them: the poor in spirit, the mourners, the meek, the righteous, the merciful, the pure in heart, the peacemakers, the persecuted. The list runs so completely contrary to our current ideas of happiness that we can scarcely believe it. Not a single reference did Jesus make to what we consider the prime essentials of happiness—health, work, adequate income, financial security, home, love, and friends. Perhaps Jesus saw from his own experience that, while the good things of life may accompany happiness, they do not necessarily produce it. The beggar on the street may be more contented than the rich man in his palace, and the martyr in prison less miserable than the tyrant on his throne. Happiness is not a by-product of external circumstances; it is a state of mind independent of external circumstances, and whether Jesus had spoken that truth or not, life itself would abundantly validate it.

Returning from Scandinavia, a woman journalist found herself sitting next to a young man who suddenly asked her, "Where would you like to live, you who have visited so many countries?" The question took her by surprise, and she could not return a clear-cut answer; but then she said, in effect, "Does it matter where you live so long as you are with the people you love and doing the work you like?" That did not satisfy the young man, who went on to say that he meant such things as the beauty of the countryside, the standard of living, the welfare provided by the state, the extent of equality and hygiene, the affluence and what this affluence can buy.

It happened that the journalist had just been to Sweden, one of the most affluent countries in the world. Except for the climate, she said, Sweden had everything—money, education, beauty, taste, peace, full employment, welfare, motorboats, weekend shacks on the archipelago, supermarkets and shopping centers, the best design for living, and excellent food. This ought to combine to make the Swedes the happiest people in the world, yet she had found them to be a discontented people, restless, bored with life, and ridden with neuroses. Indeed, it had occurred to her that the Southern Italians or West Indians, who are still struggling for the bare necessities, derive more sheer joy out of life than do the affluent Swedes.

"The happiest people I have met," she said, "are the aboriginals of Central Orissa who go about singing and dancing clad in peacock feathers; the Nagas who are fighting not against India but against the destruction of their own happy-go-lucky way of life, and finally an old fisherman on the edge of a river in Haiti, who was singing as he mended his nets." The closing paragraph of her article comes very near to the spirit of the New Testament. She says:

The longer I live, the more I am convinced that happiness is not related to circumstances as much as people think. There are many women who have little money, large families and great joys. There are many women who have everything under the sun and lead barren lives. *Where* one lives matters little so long as one can enjoy what one has, and that depends very largely on one's inner life. One's inner life itself largely depends on those one shares it with. It does not depend on the design of the furniture, the per capita income, or the freedoms as much as is made out. Perhaps even in the wastes of Siberia there are some very happy people.[1]

If we look at the Beatitudes, it becomes apparent that, while we have a right to the pursuit of happiness, yet *happiness itself comes as the by-product of a search for something more important*. In actual truth, happiness sought for its own sake is self-defeating. You hear someone exclaim in an emotional outburst, "I've got a right to be happy!" Perhaps he— or, more likely, she—has been overworked for a long time,

---

[1] Taya Zinkin in *The Guardian*, July 16, 1962.

exploited and treated like a doormat at home. You know the story. "Good old Jane. She's not married. She can take care of mother and father. She doesn't mind these things." But Jane *does* mind. For a long time the feelings of resentment and self-pity have been boiling inside her soul, until at last she bursts out, "Enough of this! I'm going to start looking out for myself. I've got a right to a little happiness in life!"

We all have a right to happiness; yet that does not alter the paradoxical fact that the surest way not to find happiness is to start looking for it. In a book written some years ago, the late Ernest Fremont Tittle offered wise counsel along these lines. He suggested that the moment we allow our happiness to become the supreme object of our endeavor, inevitably we begin to play safe and before long we are playing entirely too safe to be happy. We stop working at the point where work ceases to yield an easily purchased pleasure, and so deprive ourselves of the joy that comes from giving that has reached the point of sacrifice. We even stop loving where it begins to hurt, and so miss the supreme joy of a love that suffers long and is kind. The pursuit of happiness, said Dr. Tittle, is often an unhappy pursuit, because it engenders in the pursuer a self-concern. It defeats its own object. In our overanxiety to be happy we stop at the very point where we have our first great chance to be happy.

Look closely again at the Beatitudes. Who, according to Jesus, are the happy people? He singles them out: those who stand before God, claiming nothing for themselves; whose sympathy for human sorrow has saddened their spirits; who

16

have learned to control their strength; who seek for goodness as for food and drink; who live with their brethren in charity; who are utterly sincere; whose lives are dedicated to the promotion of peace; who have learned to suffer for the right. Plainly Jesus is saying that happiness, the feeling of inner contentment and well-being which we all seek and to which we have a right, comes as the by-product of a search for something more important. Albert Schweitzer summed up the truth of the Beatitudes when he said, "One thing I know. The only ones among you who will be really happy are those who have sought and found how to serve."

"I think I must be the happiest man in the world! I have never met anyone who has had as much fun as I have had!" What sort of man could possibly have spoken these words? A libertine, perhaps, who has run the gamut of sensual pleasure and looks back on it without regret? A world traveler who has discarded the straitjacket of convention and trotted around the globe in a kind of bohemian existence? An adventurer who has penetrated the jungles of South America or scaled the icy slopes of Mount Everest? Who is this man? Let him declare himself, for we drab, prosaic souls look with wistful envy on his exuberant joy. "I think I must be the happiest man in the world!" The man who made that large claim is a Christian missionary, Frank Laubach, whose life in recent years has been entirely dedicated to the cultivation of literacy among the backward peoples of the world. Dr. Laubach has never gone looking for happiness, but he has found happiness as the by-product of a search for something more important. Explaining his "each one teach one" method, so successfully

17

experimented with in Africa, he declared in a jubilant voice: "You cannot describe the delight of people when they first discover that they can read. Men go hysterical and women weep for joy. No other work in the world could possibly have brought me so much happiness."

The Beatitudes disclose another truth in answer to our question, Have we a right to happiness? They clearly reveal that *the secret of happiness lies in a right relation with God.* The pure in heart shall see God, the peacemakers be called the children of God, the persecuted and the poor in spirit inherit the kingdom of God. For that reason we cannot be content with a loose translation of the original Greek, but must preserve the term "blessedness" as denoting something higher than the feeling of undisturbed contentment that many of us seek. Thomas Carlyle wrote in his *Sartor Resartus,* "There is in man a higher than love of happiness; he can do without happiness, and instead thereof find blessedness." Perhaps the Spanish mystic, Unamuno, had this in mind when he concluded his book *The Tragic Sense of Life* with the prayer, "May God deny you peace and give you glory."

Jesus was a supremely happy man, and there is no doubt that to a certain extent his inner joy derived from earthly satisfactions and relationships. The creature comforts of life, the opportunity to teach and heal, fellowship with disciples and friends—all these doors were open to him. But men closed these doors one by one. All through the final months of his ministry you can hear the click of closing doors around his life, until at last they shut him into an Upper Room to face a terrible tomorrow. It was there in the Upper Room, his brief ministry a failure, the Cross but hours away, his closest friends about to betray, desert, and deny—there, in that atmosphere of gathering gloom, that he bequeathed the most astonishing gift to his disciples: "These things I have spoken to you, that my joy may be in you, and that your joy may be full" (John 15:11 R.S.V.). Think of it! Can you grasp it in your imagination—a man about to die the most terrible of deaths, talking of his joy, his gladness, his happiness? It allows of only two explanations: either the man has gone mad, or else he has fallen back upon resources of happiness about which the world knows nothing.

The answer, of course, is that he *has* fallen back on resources of which the world knows nothing. One of them is the joy which he derives from his obedience to the will of God. "My meat," he told the disciples, "is to do the will of him that sent me, and to finish his work." (John 4:34.) To Jesus there was only one criterion of satisfaction in any deed or decision: "Is it pleasing to God?" To him it mattered nothing whether the world approved his conduct, so long as he might claim the divine approval. That is what sustained him through the dreadful hours of his passion, so that even from the agony of the cross, he could make his dying breath a shout of triumph: "It is finished!"

That is the Christian answer to people who, like the stubborn, middle-aged husband in my vestry, believe that they have a right to happiness on any terms. We can only say to him, "Yes, you have a right to pursue happiness, so long as it accords with the will of God. And where do you think that the will of God lies—in standing true to your marriage

19

covenant, in accepting responsibility for the children you have created, or in deserting your family and finding solace in the arms of adultery? For be assured of this—that happiness pursued on other terms than God's approval will turn to ashes in your mouth, and you will be of all men the most miserable!"

The supreme resource of the Master's happiness was his assurance that God and only God would decide the outcome of his life. To be sure, the world had snatched all the creature comforts from him and was about to break his body to pieces; but his soul—his inner, essential self—was secure in God, and in that security he found contentment and peace. That was the happiness which he coveted for his disciples and for all who believe in him, the kind that he talked about in the Beatitudes, the happiness found even in mourning and in suffering for righteousness' sake. It is the happiness born of a right relationship with God, the faith that we men and women are not alone in an uncaring universe, but are in the hands of a divine goodness and mercy and power; the faith that God is with us, and that with him there is forgiveness for sin, solace for sorrow, strength and courage for living in all situations; the faith that history is the outworking of a divine purpose for good which holds every individual in its grasp and which, although it cannot be worked out fully amid the accidents and catastrophes of time, is ultimately beyond defeat. Let a man cling to that faith, and nothing—not even a cross—can take away his right to happiness.

**BLESSED ARE THE POOR IN SPIRIT: FOR
THEIRS IS THE KINGDOM OF HEAVEN.**

—MATT. 5:3

1 / *through humility*

Who is the happy man? Who understands the secret of true living? What is the best kind of life? How can we be satisfied and content? Poets, philosophers, and religious teachers in all generations have answered these very human questions in their own way; and we may think of the Beatitudes as the answer that Jesus gave.

Yet the Beatitudes so contradict our conventional ideas of happiness that we find them difficult to believe, much less accept. "Blessed are the poor in spirit. . . . the mourners. . . . the meek. . . . the righteous. . . . the merciful. . . . the pure. . . . the peacemakers. . . . the persecuted." What a strange list! Imagine

21

how our Lord's own contemporaries must have reacted to that kind of teaching. The Romans would treat it with contempt, and even the Jews would shake their heads skeptically. The Old Testament has its standards of blessedness. An honorable, upright, worldly prosperity; long life; cattle; crops; wealth; descendants—such, even to the devout Jew, were the minimum conditions needed to make any man happy. There are "beatitudes" in all the great world religions. One of the Chinese classics, *The Book of History,* offers a list of five Happinesses —long life, riches, soundness of body and serenity of mind, love of virtue, and an end crowning the life; not at all a bad list, yet what a contrast to that enunciated on a mountaintop in Galilee.

How do the Beatitudes measure up against the ideals of our own day? It goes without saying that they would be sneered at by that half of the human race which repudiates Christianity; but do we ourselves not tend to extol their very opposites? Take a poll of any ten people coming away from a football match on a Saturday afternoon, or any ten people wandering about Times Square on a Saturday night, and ask them what they consider essential to make them happy; and, if they bothered to answer you politely at all, it is highly doubtful that they would mention a single one of the Beatitudes. "If you want happiness," says the man on the street, "you must grab all the money you can get, avoid pain and suffering, don't be too squeamish about people who get in your way, stand up for your rights, assert yourself, and live it up while you have the chance." To the average man there would seem something laughable about the Beatitudes, something effeminate and inhuman—an impossible dream and not even a pleasant one.

Need we remind ourselves, however, that Jesus did not address the Beatitudes to the average man? To be sure, he had a comforting and attainable message for the multitude assembled on the plain, but the Beatitudes he reserved for the inner circle of his disciples on the mountaintop. The Beatitudes represented his ideal teaching, and were addressed, not to casual spectators who scarcely knew him, but to an intimate group of vigorous young men who had lived with him for a long time and had felt his redemptive influence and had caught something of his amazing power. One cynic has called the Sermon on the Mount "a consolation prize for the defeated," but the Jewish scholar Montefiore came closer to the truth when he called it "an ethical teaching for heroes." The Beatitudes describe Christian character at its highest and best. The very rewards which they offer would appeal only to a dedicated servant of Jesus Christ. The man who lives by them will be a man in Christ, a citizen of the kingdom of heaven, and as such he will find a happiness which the world cannot give, which only Christ *can* give—the happiness which is really blessedness.

Look, then, at the first beatitude. One commentator calls it the root from which all the others grow, and suggests that in a proper printing of the Beatitudes it should be a centered headline. *"Blessed are the poor in spirit: for theirs is the kingdom of heaven."*

Certainly that runs contrary to all our popular ideas. We think at once of poor-spirited people, downcast, depressed, and despondent, utterly devoid of any enthusiasm or joy. We

23

think of the gloomy man who spreads his gloom like a fog, tempting us to slap him on the back and say, "Cheer up, old fellow. Things are never so bad as they seem." We think of a fainthearted, self-pitying creature with less substance to his personality than a straw-filled "guy" which children display on the pavement as bait for pennies. "The poor in spirit"— not an attractive sort in our idiom; rather pathetic, in fact. If such people find happiness in their misery, they certainly give no evidence of it.

Perhaps some of the modern translations will bring us closer to the mind of Jesus and clear up our misunderstandings about the meaning of this first beatitude. The New English Bible has it, "How blest are those who know that they are poor; the kingdom of Heaven is theirs." J. B. Phillips, in his first edition, helps us even further when he says, "How happy are the humble-minded, for they already own the kingdom of Heaven."

Poverty of spirit represents the very opposite of all that is summed up in the word "pride." Christian theology has consistently rated pride as the deadliest of the seven deadly sins, as the root, in fact, from which all other sins grow. In his picture of purgatory, Dante places pride on the lowest terrace of all; and as the poet leaves this terrace, he hears voices chanting the beatitude, "Blessed are the poor in spirit." The late C. S. Lewis called pride "the complete anti-God state of mind . . . the spiritual cancer that eats up the very possibility of love or contentment or even commonsense." Paul Tillich, in his monumental *Systematic Theology,* traces the predicament of our world to man's *hubris,* which is the

24

Greek word for pride—not a legitimate pride in one's work and heritage, but a false pride that makes it impossible for one to converse rationally with his fellow man and, like a great wall, rises between him and God.

There is no pride more unlovely than spiritual pride, and no snob more difficult to bear than the spiritual snob. I can stand the character who looks down his nose at me because he has a hyphenated name and travels first class; nor am I particularly bothered by the superior attitude of some intellectuals. It saddens me, however, to meet a man who is proud in spirit and who obviously looks down from a great height on his weaker fellow mortals. Some years ago I helped to organize an evangelistic mission that was conducted by one of the most renowned Christian statesmen in the world. We could hardly wait to meet this man, who had been a missionary in the East and had brought blessings to untold millions through his ministry of teaching and healing and writing. The mission was an unqualified success. He preached with great power to huge audiences. His very personality mediated from the platform the grace, the peace, and the love of God. His presence was a benediction, and we sat at his feet with humble gratitude. But he would have nothing to do with his brother ministers who had organized the mission. We invited him to our homes, and he said, "I have no time to be entertained." We tried to talk with him, and he whisked himself back to his hotel. He was up there; we were down here. He had done great things for Christ, and we had done almost nothing for Christ. We knew that was true, but if only he had not made us so conscious of it; if only he had come where we are, as God once came where we are, and helped us to ascend the heights of Christian devotion and sacrifice.

A church may succumb to the sin of spiritual pride. That was the sin of the church at Laodicea, devastatingly pictured in the book of Revelation, a church so wealthy and successful that it had become smug and self-complacent, boasting, "I am rich, I have prospered, and I need nothing." It was the one church in the ancient world which included in its membership the first citizens of the community. These people were rich. They needed help neither from man nor from God. They believed that money could buy everything. The result was that spiritually they had become as poor as church mice. Their passionless religion amounted to no more than a respectable morality. Their church was not a household of faith at all, but a religious club to which the best people believed that they owed it to themselves to belong. With crude violence the author of Revelation declares that because the wealthy Laodicean church is neither hot nor cold but lukewarm, it will be absolutely and totally rejected. "For you say, I am rich, I have prospered, and I need nothing; not knowing that you are wretched, pitiable, poor, blind, and naked." (Rev. 3:17 R.S.V.) It is outside the door of this spiritually proud church that the living Christ stands pleading with the people to admit him and acknowledge their need of him. "Behold, I stand at the door and knock; if any one hears my voice and opens the door, I will come in to him and eat with him, and he with me." (Rev. 3:20 R.S.V.)

Jesus did not define spiritual pride; instead, he personified it in a Pharisee offering his prayers in the Temple. Prayers?

Prayer is communion with God. What the Pharisee said had more the character of a public proclamation. First he proclaimed what he thought of himself, and that was something really quite remarkable: "God, I thank thee that I am not like other men. . . . I fast twice a week, I give tithes of all that I get." (Luke 18:11-12 R.S.V.) Next he proclaimed what he thought of the rest of mankind, whom he divided roughly into three classes: extortioners, unjust, and adulterers—a low breed represented by "this tax collector" whose presence in the holy place the Pharisee found odious. Then by his attitude he proclaimed what he thought of God, an estimate that could hardly have flattered the Almighty. The Pharisee approached God patronizingly, as a shareholder might approach a corporation in which he owns a considerable block of stock. In fact, the name of God occurs only once in his brief prayer, whereas the personal pronoun "I" occurs five times, leaving no doubt as to where this proud man attaches the greater glory.

By the same token Jesus did not define spiritual poverty. Again he personified it, making it shine all the more clearly against the background of the self-sufficient Pharisee. Into the Temple at the hour of prayer came a publican, a despised, outcast "quisling" tax collector (the last man one would expect to find in the courts of the Lord. He had not wanted to come into the Temple, had felt himself unworthy to enter, but had been driven there by sheer desperation and need. Now he felt ashamed to approach God. He could not even look up, but attempted to hide in the shadows, with his eyes fastened to the ground. There was no doubt what *he* thought of himself, and of other people and of God. In the eyes of all three

27

he stood condemned. At length, his very soul seemed to explode, and in a gesture of self-punishment he beat upon his breast, crying out, "God, be merciful to me a sinner!"

That is poverty of spirit—not a dog-slinking self-depreciation, but man the creature standing in the presence of God his creator. It is man before the all-sufficiency of God acknowledging his own helplessness; man before the holiness of God confessing his own sin. To be poor in spirit is to be ruthlessly honest with ourselves, to approach God with empty hands asking a favor which we can never earn yet which, by his grace, he may give us.

Poverty of spirit represents the very opposite of all that is summed up in the word "pride." Yet poverty of spirit must be something more than a negative virtue, more than the absence of pride, just as beauty is more than the absence of ugliness and peace the absence of war. Jesus gives a name to "poverty of spirit." He calls it "humility," and again, rather than offering a definition, he clothes this virtue in flesh. Taking a little child, Jesus put him in the midst of the disciples and said: "Unless you turn and become like children, you will never enter the kingdom of heaven. Whoever humbles himself like this child, . . . is the greatest in the kingdom of heaven." (Matt. 18:3-4 R.S.V.) You will know what Jesus meant if you have a child in your home. You will know that he was pointing to a child's teachableness, his readiness to learn and ask questions; a child's dependence, his willingness to let people help him; a child's innocence, his simple trust of other people's motives; a child's acceptance of all men without discrimination; a child's refusal to hold a grudge, his inability to say

28

hotly, "I have my pride." These childlike qualities, before they coagulate into the adult characteristics of self-sufficiency, complacency, arrogance, and prejudice, Jesus held forth as the essence of humility, the key to the kingdom of God, and the primary condition of happiness.

No word better describes the humility of a great Christian than the word "childlike." That was my impression of Karl Barth, whom I was privileged to meet in his own home some years ago. Barth has been acclaimed as the world's greatest living theologian, the one authoritative thinker whom all Christian scholars, even in the Church of Rome, respect. His theology has become the norm, and other thinkers have achieved their stature on the basis of whether they agree or disagree with it. Entering Barth's home, I expected to be confronted by a stern, sober, perhaps even stuffy, scholar. Instead I met a winsome Christian who sat and talked with me as if I were an equal. He was as willing to learn from me as I from him. He not only laughed at the flashes of humor in our conversation; he positively giggled. And as I came away from the presence of that great man, I could only think of the words of Jesus. "Unless you turn and become like children, you will never enter the kingdom of heaven."

"Blessed are the poor in spirit: for theirs is the kingdom of heaven." We come back, of course, to the word "blessed." It translates the Greek word *makarios* which, as Gordon Powell reminds us, is the name of the present Archbishop of Cyprus. He points out that long ago Cyprus used to be called "the blessed isle" because it was so self-contained. It was rich in all necessary crops and products, and did not have to rely on imports. It had no balance of payment problems such as plague the nations today. That, says Powell, gives us a clue to the meaning of the Beatitudes. The blessed man, the truly happy man, is he who has all the resources necessary for happiness within himself. He does not depend on material possessions or external circumstances; but being spiritually linked with God, has permanent resources of blessedness which cannot be taken from him.[1]

From a purely commonsense point of view, the humble man is happier than the proud man. In his excellent book on the Beatitudes,[2] Ralph Sockman lists four adverse effects of pride. "Pride," he writes, "shutters the mind, locks the heart, weakens the hand and corrupts the conscience." We can restate it positively and say that humility opens the mind, opens the heart, strengthens the hand, and enforces the conscience. Which is the happier man—he who thinks that he knows everything and has nothing to learn, or he who constantly pushes out to new frontiers in thought and experience? Which is the happier man—he who, after a quarrel with his wife, proudly declares, "It was her fault! She can come to me!" or he who can swallow his pride and offer his love with no reservations? Which is the happier man—he who struts like a peacock, proud in his own achievements, or he who keeps himself open to criticism and recognizes how modest his achievements really are? Which is the happier man—he who prides himself on his virtue, or he who, like Francis of Assisi

[1] Gordon Powell, *New Solutions to Difficult Sayings of Jesus* (London: Hodder and Stoughton, 1962), pp. 53-54.

[2] *The Higher Happiness* (Nashville: Abingdon Press, 1950).

when anyone praised his virtues, would ask a fellow monk to sit down with him and tell him his faults? From a purely commonsense point of view, humble people are the happiest people because they have within themselves permanent resources of happiness that cannot be taken from them.

Jesus, however, spoke more than common sense. The poor in spirit are blessed, he said, because "theirs is the kingdom of heaven"; and to understand the meaning of that blessedness we must know what Jesus meant by the phrase "kingdom of heaven." To the Jews it meant some kind of social realm in the distant future—beyond history perhaps—that God himself would inaugurate by supernatural means. Jesus spoke of the kingdom as a present reality, a relationship with God that a person could seek and enter and possess, here and now. Wherever God reigns as king in a human life, wherever a man acknowledges the sovereignty of God and stands in relation to God as a subject to his king, *there* is the kingdom of God.

That kingdom, declared Jesus, is life's highest good, the most blessed state of existence into which a person can enter. It is like a treasure hidden in a field; finding it makes you surpassingly wealthy. It is like a pearl of great price beside which all the rest of life's valuables seem a poor imitation. By its very nature the kingdom cannot be accessible to the church at Laodicea or the Pharisee in the temple. He who says, "I am rich, I have prospered, . . . I need nothing," has no need of God. How then can God reign in his life? The way to heaven is through heaven, and heaven exists only where God exists, and God exists only in the heart that is humble enough to need him and receive him.

So Jesus in the first beatitude shows us a pathway to happiness. Had Jesus never spoken this truth, however, his life would still have proclaimed it. The foundation of Christianity is not a sermon; it is a Person. "He was in the form of God," writes Paul—equal with God, yet he humbled himself; he began to step down, down to the very lowest depths of humility—the frailty of flesh, a servant, unpopularity, death, a criminal's death. And when he had reached the very lowest depths, then God exalted him, and "bestowed on him the name which is above every name, that at the name of Jesus every knee should bow, in heaven and on earth and under the earth; and every tongue confess that Jesus Christ is Lord, to the glory of God the Father." (Phil. 2:10-11 R.S.V.) But see how Paul begins this sublime passage: "Have this mind among yourselves, which you have in Christ Jesus." (2:5.) Humble yourself in Christ and God will exalt you in Christ. "Blessed are the poor in spirit: for theirs is the kingdom of heaven."

Out of my smallness, my weakness, my sinfulness, and my human insufficiency, I come to thee, O thou high and lofty One that inhabitest eternity. I am not worthy so much as to lift up mine eyes unto heaven; I tremble before thine awful majesty and holiness. Yet I come because thou hast invited me and because I have no refuge save in thy goodness and lovingkindness. Whom have I in heaven but thee, and there is none upon earth that I desire beside thee; my heart and my flesh may fail, but thou art the strength of my heart and my portion forever. O God, I need thee so much more than I have cared to admit in the midst of my busy life; but here in the quiet place I drop my foolish pride and cast myself on thy mercy. Wilt thou receive me, cleanse me, empower and ennoble me; for the sake of Jesus Christ my Lord. Amen.

BLESSED ARE THEY THAT MOURN: FOR THEY SHALL BE COMFORTED.

—MATT. 5:4

2 / *through sorrow*

A woman once came to Confucius bearing the body of her dead child and asking him for comfort. The Chinese philosopher told her to collect a handful of rice in any home where there had been no sorrow. From house to house the woman went with her tearful request, and at each house the rice was quickly offered. But when she inquired if there had been any sorrow in that home, the gift was left in the giver's hands.

Who has not been plunged at some time into the universal human experience of sorrow? To be human is to mourn. Jesus wept. Even the strong Son of God shed tears of grief at the graveside of a friend. That is why we react with some astonishment to the second of our Lord's Beatitudes. *"Blessed are they that mourn: for they shall be comforted,"* or, as the New English Bible translates it, "How blest are the sorrowful; they shall find consolation." There is really no reason to suppose that Jesus meant sorrow for our sins, as some commentators suggest. We repent over our sins; we do not mourn over them. We sorrow in bereavement, we mourn the loss of our loved ones; and if life has ever plunged us into the anguish of grief, we shall remember it not as a pathway to happiness but rather as a dread detour that interrupted our happiness, or perhaps destroyed it permanently.

Throughout most of his ministry Joseph Parker, prince of the pulpit, could say that he never had a doubt. Then his beloved wife died, and in the shock of bereavement that great man of certitude wrote these words:

In that dark hour I became almost an atheist. How could I be otherwise—my chief joy taken from me—my only joy—the joy that gave gladness to everything else—the joy that made holy work a holy sacrament? O the Gethsemane bitterness! the Calvary solitude! I had sercretly prayed God to pity me by sparing her, yet he set his foot upon my prayers, and treated my petitions with contempt. If I had seen a dog in such agony as mine I would have pitied and helped the dumb beast; yet God spat upon me and cast me out as an offence,—out into the waste wilderness and the night black and starless. My feet had wellnigh slipped. Then a cruel voice said: "Renounce him! Defy him! He forsook his own Son on the Cross. Hate him, and join us, whom he derides

35

and torments as devils!" My soul was exceeding sorrowful even unto death.[1]

It does not seem possible that by any stretch of the imagination we should impute happiness to those who mourn. Yet are we prepared to jump to the opposite extreme and say, "Blessed are those who never mourn"? Such people would not love either, because mourning is the penalty we pay for loving. Indeed, the more deeply we love, the more deeply we mourn; and if we would eliminate all sorrow from life, we must eliminate all love—like the family who refuse to keep household pets because they want to be spared the sorrow of losing them.

Here is a man who never mourns. He lives all by himself in a big house on the edge of town. He left his childhood home at an early age, and does not know whether his parents are alive or dead. He has lost touch with his own family and has never married. He has no friends. He visits no one, and no one visits him. That man will never mourn. His life is perfectly insulated against sorrow. Would you call him a happy man?

Yet with full recognition that mourning may be the highest expression of love, we still cannot see it as a positive pathway to happiness. Though sorrow may not demoralize us completely, surely it interrupts our happiness like a great blanket of clouds that hides the sun for a season. That is perhaps true if by happiness we mean satisfaction with the creature comforts and joy in human relationships. If, however, we define

[1] *A Preacher's Life* (London: Hodder and Stoughton, 1899).

happiness as the blessedness of life in God, and this particular blessedness as the comfort which God alone can give, then there may be a sense in which our Lord spoke the highest wisdom from a mountaintop in Galilee.

"Blessed are they that mourn: for they shall be comforted." At the very least, they shall have the comfort of God *in* their sorrow. This is no pious platitude of the sort that we offer bereaved people for the want of something better to say; it is no consolation prize from God in return for a loss which God has inflicted upon us. "May God comfort you," we say to the sorrowful, not realizing that if God does comfort them, they will know the meaning of blessedness as they have never known it before.

A man was describing to a friend the saddest experience of his boyhood. After a long illness, his older sister, whom he had loved and idolized, died. He was beside himself with grief; and his mother, who had nursed her daughter for many months, quite caved in under the shock. Only his father remained unbowed. Though his own sorrow was unspeakable, yet he stood amid the swirling waters like a great rock to which the others clung. "I think this was the first time I ever really knew my father," said this man to his friend. "I saw a side of his nature that I had never seen before. I had always taken it for granted that he loved me, but I never knew how much until sister died. He was so tender toward me and mother, so comforting. Though his own heart was breaking with grief, yet sister's death gave him to us in a new and wonderful way."

Must we not believe the same of our heavenly Father? The Bible speaks to us of God and of how God relates himself to us—as the One who has created us, who provides for us, guides us, corrects us, disciplines us, strengthens and upholds us, a day-to-day relationship, all within the framework of a Father's love. Yet there is far more to the love of God than we can ever discover in a day-to-day relationship. There is a depth to God's love, a depth of comfort and tenderness, a recess in the divine heart which only the key of human sorrow can unlock.

A year ago I mourned the untimely death of a beloved brother-minister, a man greatly gifted in mind and heart. In his early forties he was struck by polio, and though by sheer will power and the grace of God he defied all medical predictions and returned to his pulpit within a year, it was with a body permanently handicapped. Then his elder son, an outstanding lad who intended to offer himself for the ministry, enlisted in the army, and in the Korean War was blown to bits by an enemy shell. My friend carried on with courage, but again suffered illness, this time a cerebral hemorrhage that partly paralyzed him and for a time robbed him of coherent speech. Meanwhile his devoted wife, who for years had been suffering from Parkinson's disease, became steadily worse, and after a last desperate attempt to save her life in a brain operation, she slipped quietly away. Soon afterwards my friend, then only in his mid-fifties, retired from the ministry, having drunk the cup of sorrow and suffering to its bitterest dregs. Yet the strange thing is that all this tragedy did not make him an unhappy man. He lost none of his humor, his buoyancy of spirit. Indeed in his last days he radiated a serenity and strength that seemed to come from the other world. I asked him the secret and he told me, "I have found God in a new and wonderful way. I have learned something about God that I never understood before. For years I have preached to my congregations about the love and comfort of God; now I know it all to be true." "Blessed are they that mourn: for they shall be comforted *in* their sorrow."

We can say also that they shall be comforted through their sorrow—not *in spite of* their sorrow, but *through* their sorrow. Sorrow itself will bring its own blessings; instead of being a detour from the main road of happiness, it will be a pathway to a new and higher kind of happiness. That depends, of course, on what we do with our sorrows. Tolstoi, in his book *My Confessions,* describes four possible reactions. Some people, he says, simply go out and get drunk. Others give way to complete despair and commit suicide. Still others resent the situation, stoically steeling themselves and hardening their hearts against it. Finally there are those who irrationally accept sorrow, yet stand up to it bravely and take life as it comes.

There is another alternative, however, implicit in the second beatitude. Rather than fight against sorrow or passively accept it, we can make it an oblation; offer it to God just as we offer him our money, our talents, our success; lay our sorrow at the feet of God and ask him to use it as he will.

It is possible that God may use our sorrows as a means of *creativity*. We quoted Joseph Parker's cry of anguish over the death of his beloved wife, where he told of having heard in his grief the voice of Satan tempting him to unbelief. Parker heard another voice, however, a familiar voice which said to him, "My dear, all is well; the mystery will be explained. Even at sixty-eight your work has hardly begun." " I knew her tone," said Dr. Parker. "It sounded clearly in my soul's soul, by which sign I knew that this radiant daughter of God had seen the beauty of the King. From that hour I was enabled to take up my ministry and to do the Divine bidding with a warmer zeal." [2] Those who worshiped in the City Temple in those days knew that Joseph Parker did indeed take up his ministry and do the divine bidding with a warmer zeal. Sorrow became to him, as to many of the great artists and poets and leaders of mankind and to ordinary people like ourselves, a pathway to new heights of creativity because he offered it as an oblation to God.

It is possible that God may use our sorrow as a means of *reconciliation*. In the funeral service there is a beautiful prayer for the bereaved: "Leave them not comfortless, but grant that they may be drawn closer to one another by their common sorrow." So often bereavement seems to accomplish exactly that miracle. A husband and wife, whose marriage has almost foundered on the rocks of divorce, lose a child through tragic accident, and in their common grief they rediscover their love for each other. Grown-up brothers and sisters, who have been estranged for years, meet again at the funeral of a parent and in their mutual sorrow are reconciled. In the biography of

[2] *Ibid.*

Hudson Taylor, who founded the China Inland Mission, there is a moving passage which describes the death of his eldest child, Gracie, aged eight. It happened at a critical time, when petty jealousies threatened the whole future of this work in China. Gracie's death released a wave of sympathy and love that closed many breaches. "Gracie," says the biographer, "had saved the China Inland Mission." [3] That grief itself will have such reconciling power is by no means inevitable; but God can use grief as a means of reconciliation when it is offered to him in faith.

It is possible that God may use our sorrow as a means of *compassion*. Sir William Osler, who became Regius Professor of Medicine at Oxford, was always a man of deep sympathy; but during the First World War his only son was killed in action, and after that irreparable loss, God used Osler in a new and profound way. Now his sympathy spoke from the depths of his soul. Now his handclasp became a sacrament; and his presence at the bedside of the dying, a visitation from heaven. There was little Janet whom he visited twice a day for several weeks until she died, and who looked forward to his visits with pathetic eagerness and joy. He always entered the room in a crouching position, pretending to be a goblin and asking in a high-pitched voice if the fairy godmother was at home and could he have a bit of tea. One day in late autumn the doctor brought a beautiful red rose, the last in his garden, saying that it had called out to him as he passed by and asked if it could be taken to see Janet. After Osler had left

[3] J. C. Pollock, *Hudson Taylor and Maria* (London: Hodder and Stroughton, 1962), pp. 179-80.

the room that day, the little dying girl told her mother that she understood that neither the fairies nor people could always have the color of a red rose in their cheeks, or stay as long as they wanted in one place, but that they would be happy in another home and must not let the people they left behind, especially their parents, feel badly about it.[4]

Thus God may use our sorrow when we offer it to him, and through our sorrow accomplish his own purpose of creativity, reconciliation, and compassion. If that happens, our sorrow will not be an unrelieved tragedy but will admit us to a blessedness that the world cannot give or take away. "Blessed are they that mourn: for they shall be comforted"— *through* their sorrow.

We can say also—and this is surely the meaning foremost in the mind of Jesus—that they shall be comforted *beyond* their sorrow. We must never ignore the possibility that the happiness promised by some of the Beatitudes will be realized only beyond this life, simply because it is impossible of full realization within this life. The poor in spirit and the persecuted may inherit the kingdom of heaven, but they still have to enter into their inheritance; the pure in heart will not see God face to face until they enter his nearer presence, nor the merciful obtain mercy until they stand before the judgment throne of Christ. So they who mourn must look beyond their sorrow, beyond this life, beyond history, to that comfort of God which is blessedness.

A year ago I read a searching book which was a kind of

[4] Told by Edith Gittings Reid in *The Great Physician* (London: Oxford University Press, 1931), pp. 280-81.

spiritual diary, a series of sometimes disconnected reflections written by a man in the darkness of that terrible grief following his wife's lingering illness and death. One could see the stages of grief so clearly outlined. First, the condition of shock, hitting the soul as a physical blow hits the body. Then the state of numbness where the bereaved person walks in a daze, mechanically, scarcely sensible to what has happened. Then the struggle between fantasy and reality, the refusal to believe, the insistence that the deceased is just away and will telephone any moment or come walking through the door. After that, as realization fully dawns, the flood of grief, the tears, the aching heart and sleepless nights. Then the phase of associative memory and bereavement dreams when every familiar activity brings stabbing thoughts of the dear one departed. Finally, the adjustment and the rebuilding of life around new objects of affection. This is the normal process of grief, God's way of comforting us in our sorrow. In his providence *he* numbs the soul after the initial shock; it is his way of breaking the news gradually. *He* opens the flood gates of grief after fantasy has passed into reality; *he* uses our tears as a cathartic to cleanse the wound before binding it up. *He* keeps the loved ones alive in our memory, that they may live and die again in us, be buried and raised to newness of life.

There is comfort beyond sorrow, but to find that comfort we must let grief have its full work in us. Somewhere along the way we must allow our loved ones to die, relinquish them, surrender them, give them up to God. If we cannot do this with peace and assurance, then let us look more closely at the vision of eternal felicity in the seventh chapter of the book of Revelation. There we see those whom we now mourn worshiping before the very throne of God, serving him continually, forever sheltered by his protecting care, their desires eternally satisfied, their hearts pulsing with exhaustless vitality, and their faces radiant with tearless joy. That is all we know about heaven, and that is all we need to know; for if that is indeed heaven, then it represents all that we most want for ourselves and for those whom we have loved and lost.

Yet *have* we lost them, in giving them up to God? Have they not rather become ours in a new and spiritual way? Someone wrote this beautiful prayer:

We give them back to Thee, O God, who gavest them to us. Yet as Thou didst not lose them in giving, so we do not lose them by return. Not as the world giveth, givest Thou, O lover of souls. What Thou givest, Thou takest not away, for what is Thine is ours also, if we are Thine. And life is eternal, and love is immortal, and death is only an horizon, and an horizon is nothing save the limit of our sight. Lift us up, strong Son of God, that we may see further; cleanse our eyes that we may see more clearly; draw us closer to Thyself that we may know ourselves to be nearer to our loved ones who are with Thee.[5]

"Blessed are they that mourn: for they shall be comforted" —*beyond* their sorrow. Only one thing can make our mourning a pathway to happiness, and that is the hope that one day we shall cease to mourn because we shall see our loved ones again. The author of Revelation holds forth exactly that hope. He paints a picture of heaven, not only that his readers may see the saints in eternal felicity, but that they may be heart-

[5] Quoted in *John's o' London's Weekly,* July 26, 1962. Author unknown.

ened by the promise of what lies in store for them. The great facts of their life upon earth are insecurity, hunger, weariness, death, and sorrow. Heaven represents the very opposite. On earth they shed tears of farewell. In heaven there will be no farewells, no need to weep. "God shall wipe away all tears from their eyes." (Rev. 7:17.)

That is the Christian hope. Yet more than a hope, for it rests upon God's mightiest act—the raising of his Son from the dead. The disciples in the Upper Room mourned the impending loss of their beloved friend and teacher, but Jesus comforted them by telling them to look beyond their sorrow. "And ye now therefore have sorrow: but I will see you again, and your heart shall rejoice, and your joy no man taketh from you." (John 16:22.) Their hearts did rejoice, because he did see them again. God raised Jesus Christ from the dead; and what God did for Christ, he will do for all who are in Christ. The Christian has that hope, and in that hope his sorrow becomes a pathway to happiness.

Merciful God, we remember before thee all thy children from whom death has taken away their loved ones, and who find themselves plunged into grief and loneliness and despair. Give them strength to sustain their loss, courage to accept what has happened, and the grace not to torture themselves by self-reproach. Guide them in all their decisions, and let nothing be decided under the impact of shock or self-pity. Help them to be patient and steadfast as they struggle to reconstruct their shattered lives. In faith may they relinquish the dead to thy keeping, and in love may they fulfill their duties to the living who have a claim upon them. Comfort them in the promise that life never takes anything away from us without giving us something in return; that from every loss comes gain, out of every sorrow comes joy, from weakness comes strength, and from every death comes a resurrection. Help these thy servants to see their bereavement, however tragic and sad, as the beginning of a new stage in their eternal self-discipline; and though they question thee now, may they yet praise thee who art the health of their countenance and their God; through Jesus Christ our Lord. Amen.

BLESSED ARE THE MEEK: FC
INHERIT THE EARTH.

—MATT. 5:5

3 / *through meekness*

Shall the meek really inherit the earth? If Jesus spoke the truth to his disciples on a Galilean mountain-top, then we have the answer to the burning question that perplexes the minds of men today. Never have the lines of power politics been so sharply drawn. The human race has resolved itself into two armed camps, each poised to fight the other. To be sure, some nations have nursed illusions of neutrality and have gone so far as to lecture the rest of us with an unlovely pietism, but circumstances have eventually compelled them to admit that neutrality is a posture no less perilous than illusory. It is possible, of course, that diametrically opposite ideologies may, by sheer force of necessity, coexist for a time, but that is no evidence that either side in the cold war has really renounced its ultimate goal. Eventually one side will prevail and, if the earth remains habitable, will inherit it. The question is—who?

Most of us would immediately eliminate one class of people —the meek. If critical events in recent history have proved anything, it is that it pays to make a display of strength. In the fall of 1962 Russia began building missile bases on the island of Cuba, a countermove to similar bases controlled by the United States in countries bordering the Soviet Union. When the Russian bear came this close to her nest, however, the American eagle started to hiss. She hissed so ferociously that the Russian bear decided to retreat, and slunk away with his tail between his legs. There were those who thought that the late President Kennedy should stand by meekly and allow Mr. Khrushchev to build his missile bases within "spitting distance" of the United States. But Mr. Kennedy chose to negotiate from strength, and his "get tough" policy apparently paid off. This seemed to establish the crucial importance of strength as the only effective weapon in the cold war. It seemed once and for all to have eliminated meekness from the arsenal of diplomacy.

Nor does it appear that meekness gets us very far in our personal relationships. In actual truth we pity and despise the meek man. At the very mention of this virtue our minds conjure up a picture of some timid soul shrinking in the shadows of life, never standing up for his rights, always apologizing, and too terrified to speak his own mind. In the comic strips there used to be a pathetic character named

Caspar Milquetoast—as meek as his name implies. Anyone could take advantage of him. On the street, in the office, at home, he was pushed around and trampled upon like an old doormat. His bullying wife terrified him. At the sound of her thunderous voice, he fairly trembled in his boots. Caspar Milquetoast personifies our whole idea of meekness. Such a man does not inherit even his own fireside, much less the earth.

Is it possible, then, to agree with the third beatitude— *"Blessed are the meek: for they shall inherit the earth"?* We cannot help wondering whether Jesus said it at all, or whether some later editor, perhaps of a persuasion similar to that of the Quakers, slipped it in among the other teachings of the Sermon on the Mount. Even the fact that it is a direct quotation from the thirty-seventh psalm does not convince us. In our idiom meekness denotes weakness. Meek men or meek nations are those with no guts, no backbone. Some kind of blessedness may await them in heaven, but here on earth they get dreadfully kicked around.

We had better make certain, then, that our minds are operating on the same wavelength as that of the Bible. Who precisely are the people designated by this third beatitude? In *The Higher Happiness,* Ralph Sockman reminds us that there is no English word which precisely expresses the biblical idea behind the word translated "meek," but he does suggest a number of approximate meanings. In the thirty-seventh psalm, where the beatitude originates, the Hebrew word connotes "being molded." The meek are the God-molded, those who have submitted to the divine will, who are patterned after

49

God's purposes. When the New Testament comes to state this beatitude, it uses the Greek word *praos,* which suggests the taming of wild animals. The meek are those whose wild nature has been haltered and bridled by God. Luther in his translation uses a German word which means "God-tempered," suggesting, perhaps, the tempering of metal in order to bring out its proper hardness and elasticity. The French New Testament has a very interesting version—"Blessed are the debonair," which pictures the meek man as one of God's gentlemen, polite even to those who insult him, living above all pettiness, his strength disciplined by training in good manners.

Here, then, are the meek—the God-molded and the God-tamed, the God-tempered and the God-trained; a very different class of people from the shy, frightened, cowardly Caspar Milquetoast. Meekness in the sense that Jesus used it does not denote apathy or weakness or timidity. The meek man may indeed be the strongest and most courageous of men, but his meekness resides in the fact that he does not make a show of his courage, and that he has learned to discipline his strength.

The New English Bible throws light on the meaning of this third beatitude by translating it, "How blest are those of a gentle spirit; they shall have the earth for their possession." We all know that gentleness is an active virtue. According to the apostle Paul it is a distinctly Christian virtue, one of the fruits in a Christian's life of the operation of the Holy Spirit. It is a virtue, moreover, that comes hard to most of us in our human relationships. We are naturally clumsy, harsh, and brutal, trampling upon other people's feelings like a bull in a china shop, scarcely sensible of the damage we are doing. As husbands, parents, employers, friends, we have to watch ourselves and restrain ourselves in order to deal gently with those who love and trust and depend upon us. That is the meaning of meekness—strength, but strength controlled and held in restraint.

Abraham Lincoln was a meek man, and this is all the more surprising in view of his great physical strength. As a boy in his teens he grew very fast, and by nineteen had reached a height of nearly six-feet-four. He had powerful muscles; and startling stories are told of the weight that he could lift and the force of his blows with a mallet or an axe. Men on the frontier believed in settling differences with their fists, but though Lincoln acquitted himself well in a contest of brute force, yet he shrank always from any kind of aggression. He preferred to put his great strength to other uses, such as that of saving a dog on an ice floe, or a pig stuck in the mire, or a drunken man freezing to death in the snow. Most backwoodsmen were bred to the gun, but except for shooting a turkey when he was eight years old, Lincoln would have no part in killing. Indeed, there is an early story of his protests against the aimless slaughter of mud turtles. A meek man always, he took his meekness into his home, his law practice, the legislature, and the White House. As President of the United States he could have crushed and broken General McClellan for his patronizing insolence, but Lincoln had other ways of dealing with men such as McClellan, ways of patience and tolerance and gentleness. And when his friends reproached him for it, Lincoln replied that he would "hold General McClellan's stirrup for him if only he will win us victories." Strength, powerful strength, but strength controlled and held in restraint.

It is not so easy, perhaps, to define or give examples of meekness in the policies of nations. The doctrinaire pacifist will immediately pounce on the third beatitude as a basis for his whole position, and he will ask with his usual dogmatism, "How else can we interpret meekness except as the complete renunciation, not only of H-bombs, but of all military force?" The pacifist, however, will have to find his justification elsewhere, because the Bible makes it very clear that meekness does not mean the renunciation of strength; it means strength controlled and held in restraint. If a nation has no strength, it has nothing to be meek about—in the biblical sense.

Some years ago the present Prime Minister of Canada, the Hon. Lester B. Pearson, who at that time was Canada's Minister of External Affairs and also President of the United Nations Organization, addressed an open forum at a church following a Sunday-evening service. Mr. Pearson is the son of a Methodist minister, and a man of strong religious conviction. He began by referring to one of the hymns which had been sung, "Thou, whose almighty Word," and particularly to that line in the fourth verse, "Wisdom, love, might." "Here," said Mr. Pearson, "is the ideal Christian foreign policy—wisdom, love, might. In that order. Might in the last place. Might that is necessary and indispensable in a world peopled by international gangsters, but might that is held in wisdom and controlled by love."

52

Do we understand, then, of whom Jesus was speaking when he said, "Blessed are the meek"? In considering the first beatitude we saw that the "poor in spirit" are the opposite of the proud in spirit. By the same token it might be said that "the meek" are the opposite of the aggressive. The meek have strength, but they have learned to control their strength. They know their rights, but do not insist on their rights. They have ability, but they do not advertise and assert their ability. They have grievances, but they do not press their grievances. They have advantages, but they never take advantage. They co-operate rather than dominate; they divide rather than monopolize; they assist rather than accuse; they forgive rather than avenge.

These people, declared Jesus, these gentle, restrained, meek men and nations, are on the pathway to happiness. That happiness Jesus defined in the largest possible terms, indeed the most spacious promise ever made. The meek are blessed, he said, because "they shall inherit the earth." Again we recall that this is a quotation from the thirty-seventh psalm, where the author advises his readers not to get hot and bothered about the prosperity of the wicked or to burn with jealousy against the success of evildoers. The logic of this psalm is that the violent man, the bully, eventually disappears. He is a split personality. He has something within his nature which his own cruelty affronts. And being divided against himself, his judgment becomes blind and he destroys himself. As the psalmist says, you see him one day in great power, spreading himself like a green bay tree. The next day you look for him and cannot find him anywhere. He has vanished from the scene. Meanwhile, the meek, who have been at one with themselves, their strength disciplined and controlled, inherit the earth. They do not seize the earth or take control of it; it simply comes to them as a gift and a legacy.

Surely that works out in our personal relationships. There are two ways of living in peace with people. You can bend their wills to yours, take all the fight out of them, and crush their spirits—in which case neither you nor they will be anywhere near the road to happiness. Or you can treat them as persons, respect their opinions, be gentle with them, and give their interests priority over your own. They may seem to despise you for it, and may even take advantage of your meekness, but you will keep open the channels of a normal human relationship and in the end you, at least, will be a happier person. What better example of the outworking of this beatitude than our highways? Every weekend they take their toll of aggressive drivers, bullies at the wheel who muscle their machines through the traffic, insisting on their right of way. Meanwhile, the meek drivers who have learned to control themselves at the wheel and yield the right of way, though they may not inherit the earth, will certainly inherit the highways.

Incredible as it may sound, the promise contained in the third beatitude is true. One commentator finds evidence in the world of nature, in the fact that the mammoth creatures that once terrorized this planet are gone.[1] They blundered to destruction, victims of their own too great strength; but the

---

[1] George Buttrick in "The Gospel According to St. Matthew," *The Interpreter's Bible* (Nashville: Abingdon Press, 1951), VII, 283.

sheep still graze on the hills. Do we not find a parallel in human nature? Of whom may it be said that they have inherited the earth in the sense that they have molded the life and thought of future generations? When the barbarian hordes were attacking Rome, Augustine was quietly writing his *City of God*. When Tamerlane, the Tartar emperor, swept across Asia, a boy in Germany named Gutenberg was experimenting with a rude printing press. When Germany invaded France in 1870, a crippled scientist named Pasteur wrote to a friend, "Unhappy France, dear country, if I could only assist in raising thee from thy disasters!" Of whom may it be said that they have inherited the earth?

There is power in meekness. *Blessed Are the Meek* is the title of a fascinating novel by Zofia Kossak.[2] It is a sugar-coated and somewhat spicy story of the thirteenth century, which has as its real hero Francis of Assisi. In the Christian saint we see meekness incarnate, utter lowliness in striking contrast to the pretentious and lustful extravagance of his day. At one point Francis and some of his companions were in North Africa attempting to convert the Moslems. There they encountered the last great Christian crusade facing defeat mainly as a result of its own moral degeneracy. All its superior training and impressive equipment had been swept aside by the subtle fierceness of the Saracen armies. The Christians were trapped. Only a miracle could get them out of there alive. That miracle happened. Somehow Francis interceded with Melek-el-Kamil, Sultan of Egypt and leader of the Saracens. How he ever passed through the enemy lines

[2] (New York: Roy Publishers.)

and reached the Sultan's presence remains an unsolved mystery, but there was something about this shabby little man that even the boldest and most reckless found overpowering. Characteristically Francis tried to convert the Sultan, but though that monarch was not prepared to abandon the faith of his fathers, he was deeply impressed by the sincerity, courage, and meekness of the Christian saint, answering it, as he would have answered no other appeal, with a guarantee of safe withdrawal for the beaten Christian armies.

History furnishes us with a more conclusive reason why we must take the third beatitude seriously, a reason which has been expressed poetically:

I saw the Conquerors riding by
With cruel lips and faces wan:
Musing on kingdoms sacked and burned
There rode the Mongol Genghis Khan;

And Alexander, like a god,
Who sought to weld the world in one;
And Caesar with his laurel wreath;
And like a thing from Hell, the Hun;

And leading, like a star the van,
Heedless of upstretched arm and groan,
Inscrutable Napoleon went,
Dreaming of empire, and alone . . .

Then all they perished from the earth
As fleeting shadows from a glass,
And, conquering down the centuries,
Came Christ, the Swordless, on an ass! [3]

[3] Harry Kemp, "The Conquerors." Used by permission.

56

The Teacher who daringly foretold that the meek shall inherit the earth spoke with moral authority because he himself was the strongest man who ever lived. He possessed power over people—power to change their lives and command their loyalty. He said, "Follow me," and men dropped their nets and left their businesses and their homes to follow him. He possessed power over evil: Satan could not assault him, and the demons trembled at his presence. He possessed power over the forces of nature: at the height of a storm he said, "Peace, be still!" and the winds and the waves obeyed him. He possessed power over disease and death: every illness of man's body and soul yielded to his healing touch; even the grave could not resist his strength. Such strength and power, yet so restrained and gentle and meek! He who could have entered the world as royalty came as a baby in a barn. He who could have commanded a conquering army rode into the city on the back of a borrowed donkey. He who could have crushed men into submission appealed to them with words of sweet reasonableness and loving acts of mercy. He who could have destroyed his enemies with a single stroke allowed them to lead him, like a lamb, to the slaughter.

It was the ultimate meekness, yet was it not also the ultimate strength? For who has inherited the earth? Who alone has continued his triumphal procession through the centuries while kingdoms, empires, and dictators have risen and fallen again into the dust of oblivion? The real question that will decide the future of our world is not "Who will inherit the earth?" but "Who will come closer to the way of Christ, the way of lowliness, meekness, humility?" History has shown again and again that only the way of Christ will have any future, and this, because it is the way of God himself.

In Charles Rann Kennedy's play *The Terrible Meek,* the captain of the guard speaks to Mary after Jesus' death on the Cross:

I tell you, woman, this dead son of yours, disfigured, shamed, spat upon, has built a kingdom this day that can never die. The living glory of him rules it. The earth is *his* and he made it. He and his brothers have been moulding and making it through the long ages; they are the only ones who ever really did possess it: not the proud: not the idle, not the wealthy, not the vaunting empires of the world. Something has happened up here on this hill today to shake all our kingdoms of blood and fear to the dust. The earth is his, the earth is theirs, and they made it. The meek, the terrible meek, the fierce agonizing meek, are about to enter into their inheritance.[4]

O God, my strength and my Redeemer, who hast forgiven my sins and called me into thy kingdom and made me a new creature in Christ; help me to walk worthy of the high calling wherewith I am called. Help me by thy grace to live more like Jesus Christ and to grow in his purity, his forbearance, his meekness. Give me the humility of Christ who, though he was in the form of God, did not count equality with God a thing to be grasped, but emptied himself, taking the form of a servant. Give me the heart of Christ, the tender, compassionate heart that takes upon itself the suffering of the world and pulses with love and pity for all my fellow men. Give me the obedience of Christ, his perfect devotion to thine eternal purpose which can walk the way of a cross. Bring me to maturity in Christ, until his heart beats in my bosom and his mind thinks in my brain, and I can say with thy holy apostle, "I live, yet not I, but Christ liveth in me." In his Name I offer this prayer. Amen.

BLESSED ARE THEY WHICH DO HUNGER AND
THIRST AFTER RIGHTEOUSNESS: FOR THEY
SHALL BE FILLED.

—MATT. 5:6

4 / *through righteousness*

Of all our Lord's beatitudes this one comes
closest to identifying blessedness with happiness. Most men
would agree that to be happy means to be content; it means
being satisfied with what life has given you, so that you have
no cause for complaint, no unrealized ambitions, no unfulfilled
desires. Your life is complete and full; you have everything
you want; your cup runneth over. That is happiness, and
that is what Jesus promised to the people designated by this
beatitude. "They shall be filled," or, as other versions of the
Bible render it, "They shall be satisfied."

But what does it take to satisfy us? What do most people

demand to make them happy? What are the essentials of a life that could be described as a full life?

Economic security, to begin with. We do not believe that a man who has to worry about making ends meet can be content. He should have an income adequate to his needs with something left over for the luxuries. Enjoyable work seems essential to happiness. It may not be the most creative kind, but at least a man should be able to approach it with interest and enthusiasm. Most of us crave love and friendship. We should like to marry and have children and come home at the end of the day to a place where we are wanted and appreciated. So the list grows to include such blessings as good health, leisure time, opportunities to read and travel and work in the garden, and perhaps play a useful part in the life of the community; all conditioned, of course, by the expectation that world political leaders will resolve their differences and allow us to live in peace and prosperity. Nothing excessive about these demands. It seems entirely reasonable that we should hunger and thirst after them as the very basic and minimum requirements of happiness.

The question to be decided, however, is whether the satisfaction of these basic ambitions will, in fact, make us happy. Most of us have learned from experience that rarely does life satisfy all our hungers simultaneously. These blessings of money and work and home and health and leisure time and social stability are like the pieces in a picture puzzle. We may be able to gather some or even most of them, but never do we get all the pieces in place at one time. And, should we perform this miracle, its brightness still becomes dull by our

61

haunting dread that part of the picture may be snatched away. Bereavement can fracture the strongest family circle, and political upheaval in the remotest corner of the world jeopardize our security. Are we not insulting our own nature by assuming that the creature comforts and earthly relationships alone can bring us contentment? Someone has imagined God first fashioning man and saying, "I have left him unfinished within. I have set within him longings which only I can satisfy, so that out of his hunger, his homesickness of soul, he will remember and turn to me." That so many people have been abundantly blessed with all that the world affords and have still felt an aching void of discontent shows us that it takes more than the fulfillment of our basic earthly ambitions to give us fullness of life.

Jesus looked about him. He saw the dissatisfied faces of men and women who sought happiness and did not find it in life's ordinary values, and he felt sorry for them. "You are on the wrong track," he seemed to say. "You are hungering and thirsting for things which may be worthy but which will never satisfy you. You must change the direction of your desires. You must aim higher. You must join the only class of people who are leading really full lives—the righteous." *"Blessed are they which do hunger and thirst after righteousness: for they shall be filled."*

To understand this promise we must understand the meaning of the word "righteousness." The Bible employs it in three ways. First, in a *moral* sense. Later in his Sermon on the Mount Jesus said to the disciples, "Except your righteousness shall exceed the righteousness of the scribes and Pharisees, ye shall in no case enter into the kingdom of heaven" (5:20); and to leave no doubt in their minds, he promptly launched upon a description of that higher righteousness expected of those who aspire to be citizens of the Kingdom. "The righteous," he said in effect, "are those who have learned to control their anger and their lust, who are transparently honest and kind and forgiving, even toward their enemies." Moffatt lights up the meaning of this beatitude when he substitutes the word "goodness." The righteous people are the good people, and those who hunger and thirst after righteousness are those who try to be good and right in all their conduct and in all their dealings. "Make that your ambition," says Jesus. "Try to be good and to do what is right, and you will be on the pathway to happiness."

To some ears that sounds very naïve, almost like a moralistic parent admonishing his child, "Be a good boy and you will never get into trouble"; whereas in actual truth the righteous do get into trouble. As Jesus himself said in a later beatitude, it is precisely for righteousness' sake that we may have to suffer.

I read a moving account of a United States politician, Senator Edmund G. Ross of Kansas, who went through an agonizing ordeal in 1868 during the impeachment proceedings against President Andrew Johnson. Ross held the one uncommitted vote in the Senate needed to carry the motion, and both his colleagues and constituents made it clear what he was expected to do. Ross, however, followed the dictates of his own conscience. He did what he thought was right and voted against the impeachment. As a reward he was never again re-elected to the Senate. Back in Kansas he and his family became social outcasts. "So much," we say cynically, "for the happiness that comes from trying to do what is right!"

Yet can we minimize the happiness of a good conscience? To be sure, Ross committed political suicide and alienated his friends, but at least he was able to live with himself. One can imagine him walking down the road of life, shoulders erect, unhaunted by regrets, unburdened by stolen goods, and satisfied that however the world judged him, he had done what he knew was right. It is very significant that before Ross died in 1907 much of the world revised its judgment, and even the once hostile press praised his moral courage. Modern psychology has rendered no greater service to religion than in tracing many of life's neuroses to a bad conscience. Somewhere in the past a man compromised his ideals: he cheated a relative or a friend, acquired money by dishonest means, took part in a shady business deal, or had an affair with a woman who was not his wife. He acted wrongly, and now he would give anything in the world to erase the memory of it, because so long as that memory lives in his conscious or his subconscious mind, he can never be truly happy.

Someone may protest, "But nobody is perfect!" To which we can only reply that Jesus did not say, "Blessed are they who have *attained* righteousness." He said, "Blessed are they which do *hunger and thirst* after righteousness." The sign of health is not a full stomach but a good appetite; and it is the appetite for goodness, the sheer striving to do right, that yields satisfaction. We fail, to be sure, and sometimes wretchedly, but even our failure, the fact that we are prepared to fail, is itself a sign of moral achievement. Just as the scholar, hungering and thirsting for knowledge, satisfies his intellectual appetite in the very quest for knowledge, so the man who hungers and thirsts after righteousness is in a measure already righteous. The life of righteousness is difficult, and that is why the world goes a long way to discourage it; but amid all the difficulties we find a satisfaction full and glorious which neither pain nor discouragement can destroy.

The Bible employs the word "righteousness" also in a *social sense*. This is pre-eminently the meaning attached to it by the great prophets of Israel. They knew that man is very largely what society makes him, and that righteous man cannot survive very long in unrighteous society. They knew that there is not much point in institutional religion admonishing man to be moral unless it does something to moralize the other institutions in which man has to live. A righteous God demands a righteous order of life upon this earth; and to such a God religion is a party game, a charade, unless it works to produce that righteous order of life upon this earth. Religion must make its social as well as its personal witness. On God's behalf the prophets spoke: "To what purpose is the multitude of your sacrifices unto me?" (Isa. 1:11.); "Let judgment run down as waters, and righteousness as a mighty stream" (Amos 5:24). To the prophets, righteousness meant rightness in society, and it surely had that meaning for Him who stood unmistakably in the prophetic tradition and proclaimed the rule of God among men. The New English Bible translates this beatitude, "How blest are those who hunger and thirst to see right prevail; they shall be satisfied."

No one will deny that the great need of our society today is the recovery of a fundamental righteousness. An American newspaper editor diagnosed the malaise of our western world when he wrote, a few years ago:

Something has happened to us as a people—something serious. We have gained much in the last half-century. We have lost something also. . . . Has what we gained been more important than what we lost? What is wrong with us? . . . It is in the air we breathe. The things we do. The things we say. Our books. Our papers. Our theaters. Our films. Our radio and television. The way we behave. The interests we have. The values we fix. We have everything. We abound in the things that make us comfortable. We are, on the average, rich beyond the dreams of the kings of old. . . . Yet . . . something is not here that should be . . . something we once had. Why has a moral deterioration set in among us that brings corruption, loose behavior, dulled principles, subverted morals, easy expediencies, sharp practices? What corrupts our top people in politics, business, labor, entertainment, and sport? What has taken away our capacity for indignation? What is it? No one seems to know. But everybody seems to believe it is upon us. No one seems to know what to do to meet it.[1]

That last sentence, "No one seems to know what to do to meet it," lays bare the heart of our problem. We see the moral malaise of our society and we deplore it, but we should sooner empty the ocean with a thimble than stand up against the en-

[1] Louis B. Seltzer in *The Cleveland Press*. By permission.

trenched evils of our day. People have learned to live with evil. They take it for granted that we shall always have slums and unemployment and prostitution and delinquency and exploitation and race prejudice and war; and the prophet who raises his voice against it reduces himself to the status of a tub-thumper in Hyde Park. Indeed, there is some question whether a man who takes the sickness of society as a burden on his soul will in the long run be a happy man. Will he not doom himself to a life of bitter frustration?

There is a motto which says, "It is better to light a candle than to curse the darkness"; and that surely means that we shall be happier promoting our own bit of righteousness than bemoaning the unrighteousness of the world. The writer of the 131st psalm quickens our conscience by sharing his own experience with us. He says,

> I do not occupy myself with things
> too great and too marvellous for me.
> But I have calmed and quieted my soul.

As a social reformer he may have faced the truth that many a social reformer needs to face; namely, that despair over the unrighteousness of society is just a noble form of escapism, a concern with the impossible as an excuse for evading the possible. No, he could not eradicate social corruption, but what could he do? He could conduct his own affairs with integrity. He could not expurgate the nation's lust, but he could keep his own heart pure. He could not eliminate the delinquency of youth, but he could discipline his own children. He could not put an end to wars, but he could make peace in his own relationships. He could not dispel the darkness, but he could light a candle, and in lighting it find a sense of satisfaction akin to happiness.

Not all our efforts to promote social righteousness end in frustration. Some bear fruit, and then we experience a happiness that no joy on earth can excel. I stood in a gymnasium one night chatting with the director of a club for underprivileged boys. He expressed his sympathy for these lads. "They have so little chance," he said. "Filth and poverty and crime and immorality surround them from the cradle. Their lives are all twisted, and there is nothing much one can do to straighten them." "Why do you keep trying?" I asked him. He paused a moment and then pointed across the floor to a magnificent-looking young man instructing a group of boys in wrestling. "See that man?" the director said. "Ten years ago he was among the worst of them. I wouldn't have given a penny for his chances to stay out of prison. Don't ask me what happened. Somehow we got through his thick skin. And do you know what he is today? A police sergeant. The boys idolize him." As the director said these words, I saw in his eyes something of the happiness of those who hunger and thirst to see right prevail.

A distinguished statesman once said that he preferred to fail in a cause that would eventually win, rather than win temporarily in a cause that would eventually fail. *There* is the secret of satisfaction in the struggle for social righteousness. We believe that we are fighting with God and we hope that God will eventually win. We hope, not in the human sense of wishful thinking, but in the New Testament sense of confidence in the future on the basis of those mighty acts by which God has vindicated his holy name in the past. We believe in the ultimate triumph of righteousness because of what happened on Good Friday and Easter Day. This event, as Oscar Cullman has said, was God's "D-Day," the turning point in the divine campaign against evil that guarantees God's "V-Day." Meanwhile, righteousness may lose its battles, but it has won the decisive victory, and the outcome of the war is settled. We can therefore serve the cause of righteousness, assured that what little good we are able to do is not lost, but caught up in the mighty purpose of God; and in that assurance find the deepest happiness.

Then the Bible employs the word "righteousness" in a *spiritual sense*. Paul gives it that meaning in the key verse of his letter to the Romans: "He who through faith is righteous shall live" (1:17 R.S.V.). Here it derives from a Hebrew word which means not simply "to be right," but "to be *in* the right." The righteous man is not the good man, but the man who before some tribunal, a court of law perhaps, has been judged to be in the right. Specifically, "righteousness" means being made right with God and living in a right relationship with God. As Paul sees it, God and man have been torn apart by a lovers' quarrel; and the great fact dominating man's life, though he may be too proud to admit it, and not even aware of it, is the fact of his estrangement from the God who loves him. That is why he can never be completely happy in what the world affords, and that is why he can do without

69

what the world affords and still find happiness so long as he knows himself reconciled to God.

Yet this was exactly the kind of happiness which had eluded Paul himself. With all the intensity of his soul he hungered and thirsted after righteousness. Passionately he longed to justify himself before God, and as a devout Jew, and therefore a strict moralist, he ran the whole gamut of the moral law, but righteousness eluded him. Happiness mocked him like a mirage in the desert. Then he grasped the other great concept of his Roman letter—*the righteousness of God,* which to Paul was not just a moral quality of God but a divine activity whereby God himself justifies us, vindicates our cause, and sets us in the right before him. Paul saw that we are brought into a right relationship with God by trusting, not in our own righteousness, but in God's righteousness, and that God's righteousness has been revealed and brought within our experience and made available to us in Jesus Christ.

"Blessed are they which do hunger and thirst after righteousness: for they shall be filled." Though Jesus in his Sermon on the Mount did not attach this profound theological meaning to the word "righteousness," yet it is basic to all his teachings. The prodigal son, disillusioned with life in the far country, hungered and thirsted to be right with his father. Yet he knew that it did not lie within his power to make himself right. No effort to atone, no attempt to reform, no measure of his own righteousness, could ever bridge the gulf which his foolishness had created. He must simply go home in his present shameful condition and trust to his father's forgiving love. Righteousness in the sense of right relations with our Father God is not something we can achieve; it is something that the Father himself must give.

How, then, shall we hunger and thirst after righteousness? We shall hunger and thirst by simply wanting it. That is what Paul means by faith—"He who through faith is righteous shall live." Faith is humility, the willingness to stand empty-handed before the great lover of our souls and simply *be* those who have been acceptd and justified and made righteous by the righteousness of God in Jesus Christ. There is happiness in such humility—the happiness of knowing ourselves to be at home with God, accepted, wanted, and loved in the Father's house. We may or may not possess all those earthly ingredients that make up a pattern of contentment, but it doesn't matter, because if we are right with God we have deep peace and contentment within our own hearts.

It is a large claim—that we shall find fullness of life by setting our hearts upon goodness, upon social justice, and upon a right relation with God. If our own experience has not proved it, then the reason can only be that we have not wanted righteousness enough. Jesus did not say, "Blessed are they who *aspire* after righteousness." He said, "Blessed are they who *hunger* and *thirst* after righteousness," words which had grim associations in first-century Palestine to people living on the edge of starvation.

I never knew the meaning of real thirst until I visited the Holy Land and traveled south through the endless miles of desert beneath the scorching sun. "Now you understand," said our guide, "that the secret of this country is water." I nodded agreement, licking my parched lips. At that moment, I would have exchanged all my possessions for a cup of cold water, which in some circumstances could easily have meant the difference between life and death; and when at last we came to Moses' fountain gushing out of the porous rock, I flung myself upon it and drank and was satisfied. Perhaps when we desire righteousness that much, enough to pay any price for it, we shall be satisfied, our lives filled, and our feet on the pathway to happiness.

Almighty God, who hast promised that the kingdoms of this world shall become the kingdom of our God and of his Christ; we beseech thee for the coming of that day when at the name of Jesus every knee shall bow and every tongue confess that Jesus Christ is Lord to the glory of God the Father. We pray that in this time of thy patience and our opportunity thou wilt reach out through thy Church and touch with the righteousness of Christ every part of our common life. Let our homes be opened to receive him as an honored guest. Let our literature be the kind he can read without having his eyes blurred by tears. Let our sports and amusements exalt his ideals of manhood and womanhood. Let our journalism shed its light on those areas of life of which he would approve. Let our commerce and industry be controlled by the principles which he enunciated as basic to the brotherhood of man. Let our politics be his servant for governing the people with equity and righteousness; and let our international diplomacy be the means through which he shall establish justice and peace upon the whole earth. Even so, come Lord Jesus. Take thy throne and reign; and grant that we, in so praying, may give thee the lordship over our lives; for thine own Name's sake. Amen.

5 / *through mercy*

Here is a teaching of Jesus that the simplest mind can understand. That is not the case with all our Lord's teaching. Even some of the Beatitudes seem a bit obscure until we study them more closely and discover what the scholars have to say about them. We are not altogether sure what it means to be "poor in spirit," we want to know just how the "pure in heart" shall see God, and we have to be convinced that the meek will actually "inherit the earth." But "mercy"! There is a virtue that shines with pristine clarity. The very word has an honored place in our vocabulary, and means today exactly what it meant on the lips of Jesus.

"Blessed are the merciful." At once our minds conjure up pictures from real life that clothe our Lord's teaching in flesh and blood, and put its meaning beyond any shadow of doubt.

We think of a court of law. Before the magistrate stands a young man who has been apprehended in the act of stealing money. The magistrate does not overlook the gravity of this crime, but knows that it is the young man's first offense, an act entirely out of keeping with his character, and that if he punishes him to the limit of the law, he will stigmatize his future and accomplish nothing constructive. Therefore he issues a stern warning to the young man, makes certain stipulations, and places him on a suspended sentence. That is mercy—a quality of judgment which, while condemning evil, redeems the evildoer rather than destroys him. Indeed, one might say that it is the absence of censorious judgment altogether. The merciful man hates every kind of wrong, yet toward the wrongdoer he shows understanding, compassion, and a complete absence of self-righteousness.

Our minds conjure up the picture of a battlefield. Two soldiers of opposing armies come face to face in a deserted village. They grapple in mortal combat, each knowing that he must either kill or be killed. Suddenly one of them stumbles, loses his balance, and falls to the ground. Terror-stricken, he looks up at his enemy, who is poised to run him through with a bayonet. "Mercy!" he cries, "for God's sake, have mercy!" The victorious soldier stands there frozen. He cannot kill a fellow man in cold blood, not even one who would have killed him. So he strips his assailant of all weapons and leaves him to a higher than human justice. That is mercy—to have power over someone who has injured you, or who might injure you, and to refuse to exercise that power. You cannot pardon him—only God can do that—but you can forgive him; you can refuse to retaliate.

Our minds conjure up a picture of disaster. A hurricane has struck a coastal city, reducing it to shambles, flooding the streets, and taking a heavy toll of human life. Every building left standing has been commandeered as a hospital for the injured and dying. The Red Cross nurses, who have rushed in from other communities, work round the clock, setting broken limbs, dressing wounds, easing pain, and comforting sorrow. As two of them wheel an elderly lady into a makeshift emergency operating room, she looks up at them and says through her tears, "You are angels of mercy." That is mercy —a reaching out in pity and kindness to meet the needs of one's fellow man.

> The quality of mercy is not strain'd,
> It droppeth as the gentle rain from heaven
> Upon the place beneath: it is twice blest;
> It blesseth him that gives, and him that takes.
> —*The Merchant of Venice*

Shakespeare was really paraphrasing the fifth beatitude, *"Blessed are the merciful: for they shall obtain mercy."* The merciful man, said Jesus, the man who can be charitable in judgment, forgiving toward his enemies, and kindly toward all men—that man will find himself on the pathway to happiness. And the nature of that happiness, said Jesus, is that the merciful man will himself be the recipient of mercy. The

New English Bible translates this beatitude, "How blest are those who show mercy; mercy shall be shown to them."

We must consider this truth in *our relationship to other people.* It is a law of life, as fundamental and inexorable as the laws of physics, that mercy begets mercy and that the man who is charitable, forgiving, and kind in all his dealings can expect the same treatment in return. This has nothing to do with motive or lack of motive; it simply works out that way. Later in the Sermon on the Mount, Jesus drew an amusing word picture of a man with a heavy plank hanging out of his eye, squinting ridiculously as he tried to remove a speck of sawdust from the eye of his neighbor. It was our Lord's way of illustrating the old doggerel,

> There is so much good in the worst of us,
> And so much bad in the best of us,
> That it hardly behooves any of us
> To talk about the rest of us.

"Judge not, that you be not judged," said Jesus. "For with the judgment you pronounce you will be judged, and the measure you give will be the measure you get." (Matt. 7:1-2 R.S.V.)

Morton Thompson's novel *Not As a Stranger* is the story of Lucas Marsh, an ambitious young doctor whose own brilliance and capability have made him impatient and intolerant of everyone, even his wife. On one occasion he goes to the president of the district medical association to accuse an older colleague of malpractice. The president listens to him patiently, then asks him to reconsider his charges. He suggests that Dr. Marsh should not act hastily but should remember that any man, in the zealousness of youth, judges more harshly than after he has been mellowed by age. Marsh remains adamant, however, so the president adopts a different attitude. He leans forward across his desk and says, "I am going to suggest this to you—that if you persist in bringing formal charges, then be sure of one thing. Don't ever, as long as you live, make a single mistake."

You can see at once the logic of that. Critical censure becomes its own boomerang. The man who sits in judgment on other people automatically sets standards by which the world will most certainly judge him; and woe unto him if ever he falls short of those standards. His criticism becomes an open invitation to other people to criticize the same faults in him. Because he gives no mercy, he will receive no mercy. Paul addressed that warning to the Jewish Christians in Rome. As a high-minded Jew who moved among the pagan cities of the world, Paul felt indignant to see his compatriots boasting of their moral superiority and passing judgment on the sins of society, the sins of theft and adultery and idolatry, when they themselves were guilty of these very sins. "Therefore you have no excuse, O man, whoever you are, when you judge another; for in passing judgment upon him you condemn yourself, because you, the judge, are doing the very same things." (Rom 2:1 R.S.V.)

In the second chapter of his Roman Letter Paul suggests a more conclusive reason why we ought to hesitate before censuring our fellow men. We have no right to pass judgment on them because we are men and not God, and therefore not competent to judge. Only God can judge, because only God knows the facts. He alone judges "rightly," or, as the King James Version puts it, "according to the truth."

> "Where have you been, my brother?
>   For I missed you from the street."
> "I have been away for a night and a day
>   At the Lord God's Judgment Seat."
>
> "Who would have thought it, brother?
>   For the world's heartbreaking cry
> Has risen the same from its sin and shame
>   As when you said 'goodbye.' "
>
> "And what did you find, my brother,
>   When your judging there was done?"
> "Weeds in my garden, dust in my doors
>   And my roses dead in the sun";
>
> "And the lesson I brought back with me
>   Like silence from above—
> That upon God's Throne there is room alone
>   For the Lord whose heart is Love!"

"Blessed are the merciful: for they shall obtain mercy." How infinitely more true this becomes when we equate mercy with forgiveness! It is surely strange that even through bitter experience the world has not learned the lesson that mercy begets mercy. In the slapstick of the silent films there used to be an old routine in which two comedians started to insult each other, then threw custard pies, then tore each other's clothing, and finally came to blows. It was a parable of life, of the vicious circle of vengeance which heaps disaster upon disaster and precipitates some of the worst tragedies in history.

Having brought Germany to her knees at the end of the First World War, the allied nations faced a great moral opportunity to deal mercifully with the unmerciful enemy, and so break the vicious circle of revenge. Instead, they concluded a peace treaty written in the very ink of revenge, a treaty which so drained the blood and humiliated the soul of this once proud nation, that it set the stage for the rise of Hitler and a worse barbarism than the world had ever dreamed.

We thought we had learned our lesson in 1945, but now it appears that we have not. One picks up newspapers and reads that even today, nearly two decades after the signing of the treaty, we are still tracking down former Nazis, dragging them out of their obscurity, arresting them, placing them on trial, and sentencing them to imprisonment or death. I cannot help feeling that we are making a grave mistake. Granted the heinousness of their atrocities, they were still the atrocities of war, and we are no longer at war. If they have committed crimes against humanity, then let God judge them for it. We cannot pardon them, but we can forgive them, and in forgiving take a positive step to break the vicious circle of revenge. Today certain nations face the opportunity to show the world a great moral example of mercy, and if they take that opportunity they will be directing the world to the straight road of happiness.

The truth of this beatitude may not be so evident when we

equate mercy with kindness. Far from reciprocating our acts of generosity, the world may seem to despise them. Who, indeed, has not been figuratively kicked in the face by the very people he has tried to help? Take, for example, the sailor who saved a little boy from drowning: as he emerged from the water with the child, the boy's mother came rushing up and snapped at the exhausted rescuer, "Well, what did you do with his hat?"

Yet it does seem true that the dispensers of human mercy get out of life a sheer joy and satisfaction that never comes to those who live selfishly. There is no method of drying up the wells of sorrow and disappointment in our own souls quite so effective as losing ourselves in the sorrows and disappointments of others. The happiest people are those who are always doing something for others—visiting the sick, befriending the lonely, taking care of children, giving generously of their time and money, performing what the poet called "those little, nameless, unremembered acts of kindness and of love."

Moreover, there is such a thing as casting our bread upon the waters, and by our kindness creating in the world a reservoir of good will upon which we can draw. Certainly we can create a reservoir of ill will. In South Africa two prison guards caught an escaped prisoner and beat him to death. The newspaper published the revolting catalogue of his injuries, which included fractured arms, crushed skull, damaged kidney, internal hemorrhage—and every injury stored up in the black man's reservoir of hatred which, unless it be tempered by mercy, will one day burst on the white man with all its fury.

Yet the very opposite could be true. We have such opportunity in the world today to be as angels of mercy to our fellow man. Never has human need been so close at hand or the means of meeting it so accessible. The cup of cold water given uncalculatingly and without thought of reward may not seem to profit us, but it will create for our children a reservoir of good will that shall make this earth habitable for them. "Blessed are the merciful: for they shall obtain mercy."

We must consider the fifth beatitude also in *our relationship to God*. Here, indeed, is the meaning that Jesus intended. Let us remember that he spoke, not just as a wise teacher, instructing us on the techniques of living happily together, but as God's Incarnate Son who came to enunciate the laws of God's kingdom. God requires us to be merciful. He not only advises it, he commands it; and makes our obedience a condition of the mercy that we hope to receive from him. "Blessed are the merciful: for they shall obtain mercy"—from God.

This theme recurs constantly in the teachings of Jesus. Again and again he reminds us that life is a three-cornered relationship, an eternal triangle the three angles of which are oneself, one's fellow man, and God, and that the relationship is such that from any one angle a second angle can be effectively reached only by way of the third. We can reach God only through our neighbor. We cannot love God except in loving our neighbor. Nor can God reach us or show his love for us except through our neighbor. The mercy we show to our fellow men will determine the mercy that God shows to us.

It is the theme of two of our Lord's most powerful parables. First, that of the unforgiving servant. Peter had asked Jesus, "How often shall my brother sin against me, and I forgive him? As many as seven times?" and Jesus replied, "I do not say to you seven times, but seventy times seven." (Matt. 18: 21-22 R.S.V.) Then he told a story of a servant who owed his king an astronomical sum of money and, being unable to pay, pleaded for a longer period of grace. To his utter astonishment, the king cancelled the debt altogether. Then this singularly fortunate man went out and demanded immediate payment of a fellow servant who owed him a paltry sum; and when the man could not pay, he had him thrown into a debtors' prison. Hearing of it, the king was wrathful, and he summoned the first man back into his presence and said, "You wicked servant! I forgave you all that debt because you besought me; and should you not have had mercy on your fellow servant, as I had mercy on you?" Whereupon the king reversed his judgment and threw this ungrateful man into jail till he should pay the original debt in full. Concluding the parable, Jesus said, "So also my heavenly Father will do to every one of you, if you do not forgive your brother from your heart." (Matt. 18:23-35 R.S.V.)

But the mercy we show or fail to show to our fellow men has even more ultimate significance than that. Toward the close of his ministry Jesus painted a dramatic word picture of the last great Judgment at the end of the age, when all men and nations shall stand before him in his heavenly glory to give account of their deeds. Those on his right hand will be admitted to eternal blessedness; and when they ask the reason for their reward, he will reply that, in feeding the hungry, clothing the naked, sheltering the stranger, visiting the sick and the imprisoned, they were really showing mercy to him. Those on his left hand will be consigned to eternal perdition, and when they ask the reason for their punishment, he will reply that, in failing to feed the hungry or clothe the naked or shelter the stranger or visit the sick and imprisoned, they were really failing to show mercy to him. Thus our eternal destiny will be decided, not by the doctrines we believe or the prayers we said or the church to which we belonged on earth, but by our "little, nameless, unremembered acts of kindness and of love." As we have shown mercy to our fellow men, so mercy will be shown to us before the throne of God.

It is a matter of pure logic. How else does God show mercy to us save by receiving us into his presence? And what is heaven but to be in the presence of God eternally? Yet only the people who are like God can live with God. Only they would want to live with him. Above all, God is merciful. Men discovered that truth about him long before Jesus came. They knew that in his perfect holiness he judged them, yet they knew also that it was not the judgment of a lawcourt intent on punishment but the judgment of a father tempered by love. Thus the psalmist could sing:

The Lord is merciful and gracious, slow to anger, and plenteous in mercy. He will not always chide; neither will he keep his anger for ever. He hath not dealt with us after our sins; nor re-

warded us according to our iniquities. For as the heaven is high
above the earth, so great is his mercy toward them that fear him.
As far as the east is from the west, so far hath he removed our
transgressions from us. Like as a father pitieth his children, so
the Lord pitieth them that fear him. For he knoweth our frame;
he remembereth that we are dust.

—Ps. 103:8-14

In Jesus the mercy of God was made visible. No longer
did men need to suppose or presume or hazard a guess what
God was like; they saw the whole of God's nature incarnated
before their very eyes in One who was bone of their bone and
flesh of their flesh. His perfect holiness judged evil, but
toward the evildoer he showed only compassion. From first to
last he stretched out hands of pity and help to every kind of
human need. Even from the agony of the cross he besought
God's forgiveness for those who put him there. Once the
Pharisees dragged into his presence a woman caught in the
act of adultery and asked whether he agreed that by the law of
Moses she should be stoned to death for her sin. They saw
only an adulteress, but Jesus looked through the evil deed and
saw, perhaps, a pathetic victim of circumstances who had been
trapped in sin by her own weakness and by man's dishonor.
Let those without guilt on their own consciences throw the
first stone at her; and when none presumed to be guiltless,
Jesus spoke words of redemption, saying to the adulteress,
"Neither do I condemn thee. Go and sin no more." That is
the mercy of God, and when we identify ourselves with that
woman, as many of us can, we begin to understand the depth
and the wonder of God's mercy toward us.

Because of Jesus we can change the fifth beatitude to read positively, "Blessed are the merciful: for they *have* obtained mercy." Our motive for charity and forgiveness and kindness toward our fellow men lies not in the mercy that we hope to receive from God in the future but in the mercy that we have received from him in the past. Shakespeare makes one of his characters say, "In the course of justice none of us should hope to see mercy." We are all debtors whom God has forgiven an astronomical debt. Do we still need a motive for showing mercy to our fellow men? Then let us stand on the hill of Calvary and listen to the prayer that pierces the darkness: "Father, forgive them, for they know not what they do." Let us know that here is God showing us the ultimate mercy; and let us linger here until the mercy of God so fills our hearts that they overflow with mercy toward all mankind.

Father God, who in thy Son Jesus Christ hast revealed human life at its highest and best, and who in his character and teaching hast shown us how to live as the children of thy love; grant me the help of thy Holy Spirit to be more like him whom I profess to believe and serve. Let his Spirit dwell in me more fully, driving out all those worldly tempers of hatred and envy and resentment toward my fellow men. May I have more of his charity, his patience, his gentleness, his large, loving concern for people who are weaker and less privileged than I am. Help me to be merciful and kind as he is merciful and kind. Let his forgiveness make me willing to forgive all wrong which I have suffered. Touch me with his Spirit, that my heart may be tender to all need and my hands give freely for his sake. And grant that, being rooted and grounded in the mystery of the Word made flesh, I may receive power to overcome the world and gain the life eternal; through the same Jesus Christ my Lord. Amen.

BLESSED ARE THE PURE IN HEART: FOR
THEY SHALL SEE GOD.

—MATT. 5:8

6 / *through purity*

In our normal vocabulary purity is a synonym
for chastity, and impurity for promiscuity. The brief document, *Toward a Quaker View of Sex,* published in Britain in
1963, is an informed, earnest, and extremely human treatment
of the greatest single problem that most men and women
face in their moral struggles. "Sexual intercourse," it says,
"should take place only when it becomes a consummation, a
deeply meaningful total expression of a friendship in which
each has accepted the other's reality and shared the other's
interest." This, of course, involves total commitment, and
means that the man and the woman "each cared deeply about

what might happen to the other and would do everything possible to meet the other's needs and lessen any suffering that had to be faced." Obviously there can be such total commitment only within marriage. Thus, despite the absence of any orthodox theological foundation, *Toward a Quaker View of Sex* is unremitting in its insistence that what we understand as physical purity is a pathway to happiness.

The same can be said about purity of the mind; this, too, is a pathway to happiness. One cannot prove such a statement, perhaps, but one can certainly appeal to his own experience. Let a man decide for himself which describes the happier frame of mind—a filthy cesspool or a clear, flowing river? a raging inferno or a fire under control? a wild beast or an animal that can be tamed? Of course, it is difficult these days to keep one's imagination chaste when the suggestion of unchastity assaults it from every side. One would need to wear blinkers in order to escape the impact of advertisements which show the female body in various stages of dress and undress. The very titles of some of the current films are obviously intended to excite. For a man with normal impulses it takes a conscious self-discipline to be as pure in thought as he is in behavior, but he knows from experience that in this struggle defeat leads to wretchedness and victory to happiness.

Jesus, in the sixth beatitude, however, spoke not about purity of body or mind, but about purity of heart. This includes our erotic impulses—Jesus himself said later in the Sermon on the Mount, "Every one who looks at a woman lustfully has already committed adultery with her in his heart"—but it takes in a great deal more. When we speak of the heart, we speak of the very citadel of a man's personality, the secret springs of his inner life, the motives, intentions, and affections which God alone can see. Purity of heart suggests not only a heart cleansed of lustful thoughts, but a heart cleansed of everything impure and unworthy.

The human heart may indeed be impure. Even without conscious hypocrisy a man may harbor thoughts, ideas, motives, and affections which are not quite so genuine as those displayed to the world. We have a way of describing such a man. We say that he is not sincere. The word comes from the Latin *sincerus,* a combination of two words: *sine,* meaning "without"; and *cera,* meaning "wax"— honey without wax, honey separated from the wax, pure honey. The sincere man is as pure as honey—clear, transparent, and unadulterated. But where can we find such a man? Indeed, could such a man survive in our sophisticated and competitive world? Actors in Greek dramas used to wear masks in order to conceal their true personalities. We also wear masks for the same reason—expressing emotions we do not feel, conveying intentions we do not mean, reflecting ideals we do not hold—masks designed to make people think that we are other than we really are. We should be lost without our masks; we have worn them since we were children.

Perhaps, then, we ought to look at a child in order to learn what it means to be pure in heart. No single word more aptly describes the inner life of a toddler than the word "guileless." He lives in a completely transparent world. The doors and windows of his personality are always wide open. He trusts everyone and expects everyone to trust him. He means what he says and says what he means. He has not yet learned to deceive, because he sees no need to deceive. It becomes a bit embarrassing when he tells the next-door neighbors that mummy dyes her hair, after mummy has been trying to conceal that very fact from the next-door neighbors. That a child is so guileless, however, may be the reason that Jesus held up the childlike heart as the only valid passport into the kingdom of heaven.

> Heaven lies about us in our infancy!
> Shades of the prison house begin to close
> Upon the growing boy.

So writes the poet Wordsworth of the inevitable disenchantment that takes place in the human heart, its transition from innocence to guile and from purity to deceit. How rare is the guileless person, the completely sincere, transparent man whose heart is as pure as the heart of a child! Jesus pointed to such a man at the outset of his ministry. Of Nathaniel he said, "Behold an Israelite indeed, in whom is no guile" (John 1:47). When Philip found Nathaniel and told him that Jesus of Nazareth was the promised Messiah, Nathaniel replied with his usual bluntness, "Can there any good thing come out of Nazareth?" (1:46). Yet when Jesus answered one simple question, Nathaniel required no further proof, but burst out in childlike faith, "Rabbi, thou art the Son of God; thou art the King of Israel" (1:49). This man, this straightforward, sincere, transparent man, Jesus designated as "an Israelite . . . in whom is no guile."

91

Should we still doubt what purity of heart means, then let us look beyond the teaching to the Teacher himself. Had his lips never spoken the Beatitudes, his life would still have proclaimed them. Most men employ what they are pleased to call "tact"—which is a way of justifying their double-talk. But Jesus was one man who never dealt in double-talk, a man who did not think one thing and say another. The words from his mouth, addressed to friends and enemies alike, always echoed the sentiments of his heart. Most people, notably politicians, can change their opinions as a chameleon changes the color of its skin. But from first to last, before sinner and saints, peasants and philosophers, rich and poor, great and small, Jesus never wavered in the truth that he taught. Some people are phonies, like coins that hit the pavement with a dull, metallic sound; but the character of Jesus rang true, and men saw it as gold—pure, unadulterated, unalloyed gold.

Without any reference to religion at all, purity of heart is a pathway to happiness. The guileless man may seem to get kicked around a bit, but in the end he is a happier man for his sincerity. Nothing makes us more miserable than having to keep up a pretense. Terence Rattigan's play *Separate Tables* is the story of a small and very proper hotel in Bournemouth. Among the permanent guests is a retired army major who talks and acts and dresses too much the part, and by his constant recital of war experiences makes himself a crashing bore. He commits certain indiscretions, however, as a result of which it becomes common knowledge that he is not a major retired from a fashionable regiment, but a lieutenant retired from the signal corps, and that he never did, in fact, see any real action in the war. His disgrace is complete; and when in the presence of a young lady he instinctively falls into the old routine, he checks himself and says pathetically, "No need of that now," realizing how much happier he would have been if he had been honest with her and with everybody else from the very start.

Jesus, however, promised the pure in heart a higher than human happiness. He talked of "blessedness," and in this instance, the supreme blessedness—a transforming vision of God. *"Blessed are the pure in heart: for they shall see God."* It is an immense promise, so large in scope that we wonder how it can be possible of fulfillment. We think that a man has reason to boast when he has seen the Queen of England or the President of the United States, but if he says, "I have seen God," we shake our heads doubtfully and dismiss him as a religious eccentric. The Fourth Gospel tells us that no man has seen God at any time, and the ancient Jews had a saying that no man can see God and live. How, then, can the sixth beatitude be true?

Need we remind ourselves that there is more than one kind of vision, and that we use the verb "to see" in different ways? Two children meet, and one of them asks, "Did you see the mayor's procession?" That is physical vision. Painstakingly a professor explains a problem of mathematics, and suddenly the student smiles and says, "Yes, I see." That is mental vision. At the end of the day a man comes home from work quieter than usual, and though his wife asks no specific questions, she speaks tenderly because she understands the difficulties he has been facing. That is seeing with the heart.

We talk of seeing through somebody or of seeing into a situation or of seeing back over history, and while that makes no sense optically, it makes a great deal of sense as an act of intuitive understanding.

In that sense the pure in heart shall "see God." To see God means to have a sense of God in all the circumstances and relationships of life. It means to look upon the beauty of nature and to say with Elizabeth Barrett Browning that "earth's crammed with heaven, and every common bush afire with God." It means to study history and see it, not as a blind, mechanical process, but as the continuous story of God with man and man with God. It means to look at the eyes of a child or a mother's sacrificial love or a deed of nobility and courage and recognize God in them; to find, as the poet Walt Whitman found, letters on the streets, each signed with God's name. Jesus saw God in that way. He saw all of life as a parable of God. Everything spoke to him of the divine—the birds of the air, children at play, laborers in the vineyard, women at their work, a shepherd seeking his sheep. Even on the cross, when all around him was chaos and sin, and when the agony of approaching death racked his body and soul, his lips could still frame the words, "Our Father."

Does it matter that we see God in all the circumstances of life? Does anything else matter? Until we see God, life has no rational meaning. However we interpret God and his sovereignty and providence and love, it is still the only intelligible explanation of the universe. It alone guarantees that the world is not an orphanage, life not a ghastly mistake, and death not a dead end. Never did it matter more than it does today that we should be able to look out on the fearsome, turbulent events of modern history and see in them evidences of both the judgment and the mercy of God. All of us in our personal lives run into situations so lonely and sorrowful that they break our spirits unless we see them as a meeting place with God.

Some years ago I went many times to visit a woman, a brilliant child psychologist, who spent four months flat on her back in hospital. Her illness had been of the recurring kind that dated back to her youth. Friends predicted that she would never walk again, and some believed that she would not live for long. Nothing in her attitude suggested that, however. I found her always radiantly cheerful, surrounded by books and papers at which she was working, and absolutely certain of at least temporary recovery. "I feel no fear," she said. "Even before I was five years old my parents had taught me one thing: God is beside us always, and we need never be afraid." Then she told me that never once during those months of sickness had she prayed for herself. She knew that others were praying for her, but she did not pray for herself, "lest I go," she said, "against some larger plan which God has for me." In her crisis of weakness and pain she saw God, and in seeing him, found even there a pathway to happiness.

"Blessed are the pure in heart: for they shall see God." That is not to say that sincerity alone will sensitize our spiritual vision to evidences of God in all the circumstances of life. The atheist may be quite sincere and still not see God, nor even want to see him. The childlike sincerity that opens the eyes of the heart to the wonder and glory of the eternal must

95

be a certain kind of sincerity; it must be sincerity, frankness, candor, and honesty with God himself.

This may be the very sincerity that some of us lack. It is possible to be religious and not see God, just because it is possible to be religious and at the same time not be perfectly sincere with God. The Pharisees of our Lord's day failed at that point. They were good men, they kept the commandments, they achieved righteousness in its legal sense, but their characters had an unmistakable flaw in them. They were not sincere. They welcomed only such truth as coincided with their own views, only such teaching as conformed to their own prejudices. They were religious, but religious with mixed motives. They approached God with something less than complete honesty. They worshiped God only for what they could get out of him; therefore they did not see God. Even when the Incarnate God stood before them in the person of Jesus Christ, they did not recognize him, but abused him, outlawed him, and crucified him as a heretic. Little children, men possessed with demons, publicans and harlots saw in Jesus what the Pharisees failed to see, because the very young and the very sinful, despite all their immaturity and wickedness, at least possessed hearts free from hypocrisy.

There is a searching prayer in the fifty-first psalm: "Behold, thou desirest truth in the inward being" (R.S.V.). Tradition ascribes this psalm to David, King of Israel, and its mood of penitence to the folly of his own fleshly greed. He had committed adultery with the wife of one of his military officers, had arranged to have her husband murdered, and then had married her. At once the judgment of God descended upon

Israel. The heavens withheld their moisture, and drought turned the land sere. King and people prayed in anguish. Why had God punished them so? Who had angered him? Then came the dramatic interview between David and the prophet Nathan. Subtly the prophet related his homely parable about the rich man possessing many flocks who cruelly expropriated a single little ewe lamb belonging to a poor neighbor. David, his wrath kindled, thundered forth, "Such a man should be punished! Who is he?" And Nathan, pointing a condemning finger, cried, "Thou art the man!" And David looked at himself and, for the first time, faced the truth about his enormous crime. As he stumbled into the sanctuary, the flood waters of guilt burst through his dammed-up deceit, and in absolute moral honesty he laid bare his soul before God.

We also may have to go through such a soul-shattering experience before the religion that we now find so tame and tasteless matures into a firsthand, vital, redeeming vision of God. We wonder, perhaps, why prayer dies on our lips, and the Bible communicates no living Word, and sermons have a hollow ring, and the Sacrament seems a pious pantomime, and the whole practice of Christianity leaves us cold. The reason may be the impurity of our hearts. We have not been honest with God, not told him everything about ourselves, the worst as well as the best; and until we change all this, until we love God for his own sake, and not for what we expect him to give us, until we achieve truth in the inward being, the vision of God will elude us. In Thomas Costain's novel *The Silver Chalice,* when Basil, the hero, first sets eyes on the cup of the Last Supper, he sees only a cheap-looking, dented silver mug. He goes through the experience of "conversion," and looks at the cup again, this time seeing a magnificent chalice brilliant with the light of heaven. What the heart sees depends upon the heart's condition; and if the heart would see God, then, according to Jesus, the heart must be pure.

Is there not an even more glorious sense in which the sixth beatitude may come to fulfillment? In the closing chapter of the Bible, the inspired author of the book of Revelation describes the eternal joys of the saints before the throne of God (22:4). Such felicity will be theirs, and no higher blessedness than this: *"They shall see his face."* Throughout this life we see God through the eyes of faith. Beyond this life we shall be given the blessedness for which our hearts yearn, because the veil of mystery will be removed, and we shall see God face to face. In that hope we are blessed, and in that very hope we strive to purify our hearts. "Blessed are the pure in heart: for they shall see God."

O Lord our God, who art exalted far above the earth, yet who hast condescended to our low estate and revealed thyself in Jesus; I confess that only the uncleanness of my heart has made me insensitive to thy presence in the midst of life. Thou hast commanded me to seek thy face, and I have answered, "Thy face, Lord, will I seek"; but my vision has been dull and my ears deaf, and I have not known thee, though thou didst come near and speak to me. If the pure in heart shall see God, wilt thou, by the power of thy Holy Spirit, cleanse my heart of all insincerity, all pretense, all hypocrisy, everything that comes like a great cloud between me and thee. Open my eyes to see thee in all that thou hast created, and to recognize thy presence in joy and in sorrow and in all the duties and relationships of life. If little children have eyes to discern thy beauty, give me the childlike mind, that I may behold thy glory in the face of Jesus Christ. Even now, as I kneel before thee in prayer, wilt thou grant me a vision of thyself, that I may worship thee in the beauty of holiness, that I may go back into the world never again to lose sight of thee, and that when at the last thou dost summon me into thy nearer presence, I shall behold thee in thine eternal splendor; through the merits and mediation of Jesus Christ my Lord. Amen.

7 / *through reconciliation*

Today we are faced with the pre-eminent fact that, if civilization is to survive, we must cultivate the science of human relationships—the ability of all peoples, of all kinds, to live together and work together, in the same world, at peace.

So declared Franklin D. Roosevelt, President of the United States, on the night before he died, and who would doubt that he spoke the truth? Today the whole world is unanimous in pointing to peace as a pathway to happiness. In a radio interview the question was put to a worker among refugees: "How much longer do you think the refugee problem will continue?" He replied, "Until the world

100

achieves peace." So many of the human problems that remain to be solved before large masses of the world's population can be redeemed from misery are predicated on the absence of peace. Not that peace itself will mark the fulfillment of all our utopian dreams, but peace is certainly a pathway to them. There may have been a day when the world heaped its highest honors on the makers of war, leaving the peacemaker to walk a lonely, unpopular path; but modern science, with its horrifying methods of mass annihilation, has changed all that. Today we acclaim the makers of peace as our saviors, knowing that either they must succeed, or else we shall all be blown up. As for the peacemaker himself, his task leads to happiness because his fate is bound up with that of other men, and upon the success of his efforts his own survival depends.

Jesus, however, in the seventh beatitude, promised that we shall find happiness in the very *act* of making peace. He promised that the man who actively tries to reconcile conflicting parties, be they individuals, classes, races, or nations, will himself experience a sense of joy and satisfaction that never comes to those who simply long for peace or even pray for it.

Who, then, are the peacemakers? Who are the men or the groups of men actively engaged in reconciliation? This is the question that must absorb our thoughts as we try to understand this verse from the Sermon on the Mount. Whom did Jesus designate in the seventh beatitude when he said, *"Blessed are the peacemakers: for they shall be called the children of God"*?

Assuredly he designated *the people who have achieved peace in their own relationships*. Could anything be more inconsistent than a marriage counselor attempting to reconcile estranged husbands and wives, when his own home is torn apart by friction and misunderstanding? Could anything be morally weaker than a nation attempting to mediate in a dispute between other nations, when it stands from day to day in a posture of war? Obviously, peacemaking begins with oneself. Before you can be effective in helping other people to resolve their differences you must be a man of peace who, as Roosevelt said, has cultivated "the science of human relationships."

Abraham was such a man. When he and his nephew Lot came as immigrants to the region of Bethel, they were so wealthy, each possessing so many herds and flocks and tents, that they found that the area was not big enough to support them both. As usual, this problem of overpopulation created tensions, and we read that "there was strife between the herdsmen of Abram's cattle and the herdsmen of Lot's cattle" (Gen. 13:7 R.S.V.). Despite his seniority in age and in rank, Abraham dealt with the problem in a statesmanlike way. He said to Lot, "Let there be no strife between you and me. . . . Is not the whole land before you? Separate yourself from me. If you take the left hand, then I will go to the right; or if you take the right hand, then I will go to the left." (13:8-10 R.S.V.) Interpreting this magnanimity as softness, Lot naturally chose to settle in the lush Jordan Valley, leaving the less fertile mountainous area to his uncle, leaving him also, however, to inherit the proclaimed blessing of God.

What a miraculous easing there would be in world tensions if groups now hostile to one another could overcome their pride sufficiently to speak as Abraham spoke; if the white and black races in Africa could meet on an equal footing and say, "Let there be no strife between you and me"; if management and labor could sit at the conference table and say, "Let there be no strife between you and me"; if East and West could come together in the United Nations and say, "Let there be no strife between you and me."

Paul, in one of his great moral exhortations, wrote to the Christians at Rome, "If possible, so far as it depends upon you, live peaceably with all" (Rom. 12:18 R.S.V.). Clearly the apostle recognized that however conciliatory we may be, we cannot live harmoniously with *all* people, because some are determined to be our enemies and they stubbornly spurn our efforts at reconciliation. As Christians, however, we are bound to remove all causes of enmity, insofar as those causes are rooted in our own pride. We all have our conflicts at home, at work, and in the neighborhood; and though we may not admit it or even be aware of it, these conflicts do damage to our personalities. More than one psychiatrist, in helping a patient to analyze his neuroses, has traced the cause to a long-standing and deep-seated enmity, perhaps between the patient and one of the members of his own family, and has said, "Until you resolve this conflict, you will never be completely well." So often the pathway to happiness lies in saying to a person whom you have hated and resented and tried to avoid, "Let there be no strife between you and me."

Then it can be said that the peacemakers are *people actively engaged in trying to remove the causes of strife.* In a small village there were two brothers who would have no dealings with each other. On the street they passed as strangers, and the quarrel extended even to their children and grandchildren. It was a rather primitive rural area, without many of the modern conveniences, and the dispute had to do with water rights, a creek that generated electric power for one brother to run his sawmill and the other brother his gristmill. Each laid exclusive claim to the water supply, and neither seemed capable of making any compromise agreement. The dispute lasted for years. One day progress caught up with the little village. An electric company installed poles and wires and brought in enough commercial power for the whole community to light its homes and run its mills, so for this purpose the waters of the creek were no longer needed. It took some time for reality to sink in, but eventually the two brothers did become reconciled because they realized that the cause of their strife had been removed.

Peacemakers are the people who work to remove the causes of strife. Unhappily, that does not always include those who call themselves "pacifists." It may include some pacifists, especially the high-minded ones who find their motives in Christian obedience, and not simply in the fear of being blown up. There is a world movement, with its headquarters in England, known as The Fellowship of Reconciliation. It started with two men, an Englishman and a German, who shook hands on the station platform at Cologne on the eve of the First World War and vowed that, however long and fierce the strife between their two countries, nothing would destroy their fellowship in Christ. Those who belong to the Fellowship of Reconciliation are pacifists by conviction, with all that doctrinaire pacifism implies, but nonresistance is only the negative side of their Christian obedience; positively, they obey the command of Christ to reconcile people, making peace between them by trying to remove the causes of strife.

Some pacifists do everything except make peace between people, and I am not referring solely to the beatnik variety who express their personalities by creating a public disturbance. I am referring also to those who have so much to say about "love" and then display a strangely militant, dogmatic, intolerant, and downright belligerent attitude toward any who do not agree with them. Not long ago I was invited to a meeting intended to bring together some pacifists and nonpacifists with a view to finding a common Christian approach to the problems of achieving peace. One of the pacifists refused to come, and sent a letter of apology in which he said that he could see no point in such a meeting. There was nothing to discuss anyway. Either the Christian ethic demanded nonviolence or it did not; and if it did, then any compromise would be a covenant with hell. So often that is where the pacifist stands. He does not believe that there can be any other Christian position. He alone is the truly consistent Christian; the rest of us have read the Gospels imperfectly. He will never recognize that our agony of soul might be just as great as his, and that we who believe that we should defend not only our homes and families but the human values for which other men have died, are also acting from the motives of Christian obedience.

In a religious periodical I came across an article written by a man who contended quite sincerely that if you want to find real Christianity today, do not look for it in the smug, stuffy churches, but in the disreputable fringe movements and especially in the Campaign for Nuclear Disarmament. That point of view tells me more about the author than about Christianity, and prompts me to ask: Without bringing religion into it—if so many young men and women today feel passionately the futility and the evil of war, then why do they not lend their strength to those movements in our society that work to remove the causes of war? Poverty! The gross inequality that still exists between the very rich and the very poor. Homelessness! Nearly five thousand without a roof over their heads in London; two mothers thrown out in the street by thugs hired by the landlord. Racial persecution! Neo-Nazi movements and colored immigrants forced to defend themselves with knives. Let our angry young enthusiasts turn their energies to the eradication of strife-producing problems such as these. The true peacemakers today are not those who sit down in the road and block traffic, but those who employ another part of their anatomy, their hands, packing bundles of food and clothing for refugees and reaching out to help the victims of misery, removing the causes of tension, so that men shall no longer have reason to fight one another.

On the island of Samoa there is a very famous road known as "the Road of the Loving Heart." The natives built it to link their village with the home of a beloved friend, Robert Louis Stevenson; and they presented it to him just before he died. When Stevenson came to the island, he found the natives in a state of perpetual war, fighting and killing one another. By teaching them to live decently, he removed many of the causes of their strife, and in making peace among them found his own highest happiness.

The peacemakers are also *those who build bridges of understanding.* In 1961 the Communists built the Berlin wall, that bulwark of stone, mortar, and barbed wire which isolates two million West Berliners from their surrounding East German kinsmen. Nearly eight miles long, it consists of enough concrete slabs to build homes for 150 families. On 358 occasions East German border guards have fired on escaping refugees; more than once they have left a victim to bleed to death.

The Berlin wall is really much older and longer than one political crisis. It symbolizes a spirit and a mentality. It is an outward and visible sign of the cold war, a mark of humanity's division, mistrust, and fear. High and wide, visible and invisible, it meanders through every country, every society, every culture, appearing one day as a cruel wall of glass through which Negroes can see but not walk, and on another day as a great barrier of misunderstanding between management and labor that threatens to throw society into economic chaos. One great fact dominating life on this earth is the fact of tension—tension between man and man, class and class, nation and nation, race and race, ideology and ideology.

We can thank God, however, that this is not the only fact in our world. Exactly a year and a day after the construction of the Berlin wall, an eight-mile tunnel was completed beneath Mont Blanc, piercing an age-old barrier between France and Italy. Linking two nations which have alternately been friends and enemies, it is a symbol of trust and reconciliation.

Tunnels and bridges—there are many of them being built today, quietly and without fuss. One of them was completed near Dijon in France as a place of worship for both Catholics and Protestants, a place of prayer to heal the breaches between father and son, husband and wife, believer and unbeliever. It is called The Church of Reconciliation—an apt name, because it was inspired by a Berlin lawyer who wanted to make expiation for the countries ravaged by the Nazis. Members of the same movement helped to rebuild the old vestries of Coventry Cathedral. For six months fourteen young Germans, nearly all from the eastern zone, worked in Coventry at less than three shillings a day, their materials and labors financed by churches, schools, and youth groups in Germany.

The great peacemakers have been bridge builders, men who dedicated themselves to forging links of understanding between their fellows. Abraham Lincoln was such a man, always the peacemaker, always the reconciler. On one occasion during his presidency, the Secretary of State showed him the draft of a rather insulting dispatch to the British Government which, if it had been delivered as it stood, would certainly have strained relations between Washington and London. That draft now exists with the alterations made in Lincoln's own handwriting. By a few touches, some of them very minute, made with the skill of a master of language and a lifelong peacemaker, Lincoln changed the draft into a firm but entirely courteous dispatch. He instructed the American ambassador in London not to read it verbatim to Lord Russell, but rather to convey the sense of it tactfully and graciously. Thus with a few strokes of his pen and a simple decision Lincoln built a bridge of understanding.

How quickly the complexion of our world would change if all politicians pleaded for understanding instead of appealing to angered prejudices. For most of us, however, it comes down to a matter of our personal relationships. Everyday life compels us to arbitrate between our fellow men, because each one of us enjoys the respect and the confidence of at least two people who cannot live together in peace. We have the choice either to fan the flames of enmity or to pour oil on the wounds of bitterness. Often just a word will suffice, a word which says, "Let me tell you something else about him," or, "I really don't think he meant it that way." Augustine wrote about his mother, Monica, that "she showed herself such a peacemaker, that hearing on both sides such bitter things . . . she never would disclose aught of the one

unto the other, but what might tend to their reconcilement."
What shall we be, therefore—builders of walls or builders
of bridges?—for the answer we give may well determine
our right to happiness.

Above all, the peacemakers are *those who reconcile men
to God*. Once a year we celebrate with exciting joy the
birthday of the greatest Peacemaker of all. On Christmas
Eve a holy silence envelops the earth, and the pulse of hope
begins to throb once more in our hearts as the song of angels
comes down the centuries: "Glory to God in the highest, and
on earth peace, good will toward men." God sent his Son
into the world as the Prince of Peace; constantly Jesus took
the word "peace" on his lips; as a last bequest to his disciples he bequeathed the gift of his own peace: "Peace I
leave with you, my peace I give unto you" (John 14:27).
In the Bible, however, and especially in the teachings of
Jesus, the word "peace" has a very definite meaning. Only
secondarily does it mean reconciliation between man and
man; primarily it means reconciliation between man and
God. Christ does indeed reconcile men who are at enmity
with one another, but only because he first reconciles both
to God, bringing them into a completely new relationship
where their enmity disappears.

It is not enough to describe Christ as a maker of peace.
The apostle Paul came nearer the truth when he wrote to the
Ephesians, "He is our peace who has made both one, and
has broken down the dividing wall of hostility" (2:14
R.S.V.). Not, "He *makes* our peace," but "He *is* our peace";

and there is a difference here, as we know from our human relationships. A man and wife estranged from each other may consult a wise counselor, who makes peace between them by advising each separately and then bringing them together in reasonable understanding. But suppose a baby is born to them, a little life which both have created and in which both share, a center for their mutual love. Obviously the gurgling infant does not *make* peace between his parents, but it can be said that he *is* their peace, for in him the husband and wife meet. So it is that men meet in Christ, men who are different racially, ethnically, ideologically, and temperamentally. Christ does not arbitrate between opposing parties. As Paul says, he creates in himself "one new man in place of the two, so making peace" (2:15 R.S.V.).

That answers our question, Who are the peacemakers? According to the New Testament they are those who go out into the world publishing the good news of Jesus Christ —the evangelists, missionaries, teachers, doctors, social workers, and consecrated Christian laymen who have a gospel of reconciliation to proclaim. Not for a moment do we minimize the great secular enterprises, such as the late President Kennedy's Peace Corps and the United Nations' agencies. There have been some great peacemakers who would hardly describe themselves as Christians and yet to whom the world owes an unpayable debt. As Christians, however, we believe that mankind will never become a family except within the fatherhood of God and that men will never live as brothers until they can live together as sons of God. That is why we believe that the decisive factor in achieving

111

world peace today and in resolving the tensions of our personal and social lives is the mission and the ministry of the Christian church. We believe that we are making our greatest contribution to peace by supporting the Church; for as God gave Christ to reconcile men to him, and therefore to one another, so Christ commissioned his Church to continue the divine ministry of reconciliation.

It is no accident that, wherever a bridge of understanding is built these days, the Church should supply so many of the materials. It is no accident that sometimes the Church has been the first and only bridge to span the barriers of man's hatred and pride. On February 17, 1942, Japanese planes bombed the city of Darwin in northern Australia, completely destroying the American headquarters on the main street. On June 23, 1960, the Japanese ambassador stood on that very spot and in simple and sincere terms expressed the good wishes of the Japanese people to the congregation of the United War Memorial Church of Darwin, which on that day was being opened and dedicated there. At one point in the ceremony Mr. Fujita, of the Japanese firm which is still salvaging war wrecks from Darwin Harbour, stepped forward to make a gift of metal crosses made from the vessels sunk by the bombers. They have been inset in the ends of the pews and in the Communion table and pulpit. The church in the Japanese city of Kyoto donated pure silk frontals for the pulpit and lectern. Woven into the fabric of the frontals are two symbols—an ocean wave and a flock of birds. They represent the carrying of the Christian gospel across the seas. With them came a message: "May this gift reunite the

112

two Christian churches in Kyoto and Darwin as a symbol of reconciliation in Christ."

These, then, are the peacemakers—the people who have achieved peace in their own relationships, who work to remove the causes of strife, who build bridges of understanding and who reconcile men to God. Can it be said that they are on the pathway to happiness? Not always, in terms of the world's standards. The way of the peacemaker may be discouraging and dangerous, and may even end in tragedy, as it did for Count Bernadotte in Jerusalem and Dag Hammarskjöld in Africa and Christ on his cross. Whoever tries to stop a fight may have to offer himself as a martyr, because only by turning upon him with a mutual hatred will the antagonists resolve their differences. Reconciliation, therefore, is not always a pathway to happiness; but we can believe assuredly that it is a pathway to blessedness. Christ promised that in the Beatitudes. He promised that people who live and work and suffer for the brotherhood of man will be so spiritually close to God that his fatherhood will be not a theory but a fact, the supreme, unshakable source of their security and joy for all eternity. To the peacemaker God will say what he has said perfectly only to Jesus, "My beloved Son!" "Blessed are the peacemakers: for they shall be called the children of God."

O God, who art a God not of confusion but of peace, we pray for an easing of the tensions that divide men today. By the might of thy Spirit help us to break down those artificial barriers that rise like a great wall between people who have the same human feelings, the same hopes and fears, the same love of peace, and the same loathing of war. Confound the designs of ambitious and greedy men who derive personal gain by fanning the flames of hatred, who sow seeds of misunderstanding and set brother against brother. Thou who hast dealt so patiently with a world estranged from thee by its own proud disobedience, wilt thou give to men and nations a new patience with one another, a new tolerance and a new sympathy. We pray for the spirit of reconciliation upon the earth, and we beseech thee that it may arise, not from our fears, but from the knowledge of thy redeeming love in the cross of Jesus Christ. In his strong Name we offer this prayer. Amen.

BLESSED ARE THEY WHICH ARE PERSE-
CUTED FOR RIGHTEOUSNESS' SAKE: FOR
THEIRS IS THE KINGDOM OF HEAVEN.

—MATT. 5:10

8 / *through persecution*

Only on the most rare occasions did Jesus ever stop to explain his teachings. Usually he said what he had to say and then left people to understand and interpret it for themselves. In his book *Into a Far Country*, Erik Routley proposes the idea that Jesus employed "the principle of trajectory," which means that he never communicated the truth exhaustively, but always with a certain reticence. He taught as a humorist tells a funny story, trusting the listener to get the point for himself. The very word "parable" derives from a Greek root *ballo,* a term used in ballistics, meaning "I throw." Jesus threw his teaching like a ball, expecting the receiver to reach out and catch it.

On a few remarkable occasions, however, Jesus did make an exception to this rule. There were times when even his disciples felt puzzled and bewildered by what he said. So not with intent to spoil a story by moralizing it, but simply to answer their unspoken questions, Jesus deliberately spelled out the meaning of his own teaching. The parables of the soils and the tares are cases in point, and so is the eighth and closing beatitude. *"Blessed are they which are persecuted for righteousness' sake: for theirs is the kingdom of heaven."* Speaking to his disciples on the mountaintop, Jesus sensed that though what he had said thus far might be plain enough, yet here was a teaching that must be enlarged and amplified if it was going to make any sense at all. Therefore he went on to say, *"Blessed are ye, when men shall revile you, and persecute you, and shall say all manner of evil against you falsely, for my sake. Rejoice and be exceeding glad: for great is your reward in heaven: for so persecuted they the prophets which were before you."*

It does indeed seem a strange reversal of our human values. We have been studying the Beatitudes as the answer given by the wisest of all teachers to the question, Who is the truly happy man? We have had to probe rather deeply in order to be convinced that such qualities as humility, sorrow, and meekness actually lead to happiness; but in each case we have gained at least a glimmer of understanding. Now we come to a word that really taxes our credulity: "Blessed are they which are persecuted for righteousness' sake: for theirs is the kingdom of heaven." Not that we doubt its truth; if Jesus spoke it, then we are prepared to believe that it must be true.

116

Still, we have always assumed that as a basic requirement of happiness a man should know how to get along with his fellows. Did not Jesus himself designate the peacemakers as happy people? And at the very least we can distinguish them as people who have learned to make peace in their own relationships. How can we live peacefully with people when we irritate and anger them to a point where they dislike us and hate us and feel impelled to persecute us? That takes a bit of explaining, so we can be grateful that Jesus enlarged upon this beatitude, showing us first what it means to be persecuted, and then pointing the two pathways along which persecution leads to blessedness.

First, let us see how Jesus defined "persecution." He said, "Blessed are they which are persecuted for righteousness' sake." He did *not* say, "Blessed are those who are persecuted for the sake of self-righteousness." All of us must have felt at times that much of the world's antagonism toward Christian people and toward the Church might be spared if Christians did not deliberately go out of their way to provoke it. When our dogmatism turns us into intellectual bullies; when our virtuousness makes us moral prigs; when we become intolerant and disputatious; when we are everlastingly arguing, criticizing, and rebelling, of course we shall get ourselves disliked and of course we shall be persecuted in varying degrees. Unhappily, some Christians have a perverted streak in their nature which enjoys this and derives from it a sense of morbid satisfaction. They want to be unpopular because it makes them feel morally superior and proves to them that

117

they really are Christians, different from other people, like the snobbish Pharisee who prayed in the temple, "God, I thank thee, that I am not as other men are."

This was the theme of *Family Portrait,* a play that appeared some years ago, and which told the story of a working-class English family, quite respectable but altogether unchurched, except for one daughter who had "got religion" at an evangelical meetinghouse. It was more a religion of the Old Testament than of the New, because instead of making her sweeter and more loving toward the members of her family, it made her intolerant and critical. The others minced no words in telling her what they thought of her religion, but she didn't mind; in fact she welcomed their abuse. And just to make sure that she drove all of them mad, she ended every argument by retreating to her bedroom to sing gospel hymns in a loud, unmusical voice.

But surely nothing could be further from the happiness that Jesus promised in the Beatitudes, the happiness conferred by God on those who live according to the rules of his kingdom. This happiness, declared Jesus, comes only to those who are persecuted *for righteousness' sake.* The man who tries to do what is right, in his behavior and in all his dealings, the man who dedicates himself to the promotion of right relations in human society, is bound to make enemies. There will always be people who resent him and hate him and in some degree try to persecute him. What that means can be seen very clearly in the history of our faith and in the experience of righteous men.

For righteousness' sake a man may lose his reputation,

because the world will indeed revile him and persecute him and say all manner of evil against him falsely. One of the more subtle methods which the ancient world employed to get rid of the Church was to spread lies about it. They accused the early Christians of being atheists, homosexuals, subversives, and traitors to the state. The situation has not changed greatly. Today the university student or the office worker who joins his colleagues in a discussion about religion will listen to some very baseless and cutting criticisms about the evils of Christianity and the hypocrisy of Christians. It takes a great deal of moral courage for him to stand his ground and maintain his Christian witness under the pressure of this subtle persecution.

For righteousness' sake a man may lose his friends. Ibsen wrote a powerful play called *Enemy of the People,* about a public health officer who, because he exposed a social evil in the community, found himself deserted by the city fathers, by public opinion, by his friends, and at last by the members of his own family, until he stood quite alone. That can be the fate of any man in any profession who stubbornly stands for what he believes to be right. The Christian family who make it plain that they support the Church and send their children to Sunday school and keep the sabbath may find that they live as strangers in their own neighborhood. Other families quickly establish a pattern of free fellowship, but the Christians are so often the odd penny; they stand on the outside looking in and even the children have to bear the brunt of this unconscious persecution.

For righteousness' sake a man may lose his security. In many

Communist countries today the authorities no longer persecute the Church; they simply make the position of Christians economically intolerable. In East Germany, a teacher in a state school, who has a family of three children, will receive from the state about one thousand marks a month—enough to live in comparative comfort. Should he teach in a church school, he would receive less than one quarter of that amount —enough, perhaps, to purchase one pair of shoes of the poorest quality. It is not uncommon in our own society for a man to be forced to resign his job because he will not connive at business practices which fall beneath the level of Christian morality; or for a woman to complain that her employer has made her position a living hell because he resents the Christian influence of her character.

For righteousness' sake a man may even lose his life. That great world building, the Colosseum in Rome, scene of savagery and death, stands as the fit and enduring symbol of what it cost the early Christians to maintain the integrity of their faith. And in Britain there are monuments which keep alive the memory of men and women who stood firm for righteousness' sake and paid the ultimate price for their convictions. Today, under psychological torture, men pay an even more terrible price—the loss, not of life itself, but of the freedom to die as martyrs; the loss of reason, will, dignity, and personal identity. We need not probe beneath the surface of human history and human experience to know what it means to be persecuted for righteousness' sake.

In the light of this rather grim analysis it become even more difficult for us to understand just how persecution, physical or psychological, can possibly be a pathway to happiness. How can we describe a man who has lost his reputation, his friends, his security, or his life as a happy man? Perhaps we cannot, in terms of the world's standards; yet even on these terms the experience of some Christians has been quite remarkable. In his Yale Lectures[1] Gerald Kennedy writes of listening to a man who had been one of the leaders of the Norwegian underground during the Nazi occupation as he described some of his experiences during that harrowing period. He told about the narrow escapes, the constant danger, the threat of torture, and the exhausting tasks. Then he said in a kind of wonderment that one day it came to him that he was what men would call a happy man. In those perilous circumstances, marked by the absence of everything that we count requisite to happiness, this man had experienced something of the deep contentment and satisfaction that we all crave.

Let us look more closely at the teachings of Jesus. He said, "Blessed are they which are persecuted for righteousness' sake"; and then he went on to suggest two specific reasons why persecution may be called a pathway to happiness. First, because it admits us to a glorious company. "Rejoice, and be exceeding glad: . . . for so persecuted they the prophets which were before you." There can be no doubt that the prophets suffered persecution. We think of Elijah driven into the wilderness by a wicked queen who sought to take his life; and of Amos forbidden under penalty of death to preach in the city; and of Jeremiah placed in the stocks and later

[1] *God's Good News* (New York: Harper & Row, 1955), p. 46.

121

lowered by ropes to await death in a dark, dank, mucky cistern. It may seem a lonely business to maintain the grandeur of independent integrity, but if a man who is persecuted for righteousness' sake looks back over history he will see himself to be a part of the most creative and courageous company that the world has ever known.

There is one striking difference between an audience of modern Christians and the little handful of disciples who first listened to the Beatitudes on a mountaintop in Galilee: these men stood on the very threshold of persecution. In a matter of months it would become the supreme fact dominating their lives; and here was Jesus telling them not simply to be prepared to confront it, but to welcome it with abounding joy. They did exactly that. We see the familiar pattern in the fifth chapter of Acts. For spreading the gospel of Christ the disciples were thrown into prison. Next day the religious authorities brought them before the council, warning them that unless they desisted from preaching, they would be put to death. Stubbornly Peter retorted, "We must obey God rather than men." (5:29.) Had it not been for the wise caution of Rabbi Gamaliel, some of the pharisaic hotheads would have killed the disciples there and then. Instead they administered a severe beating, and we read that, with blood oozing from their backs, the disciples "left the presence of the council, rejoicing that they were counted worthy to suffer dishonor for the name" (5:41).

Again and again that pattern has been repeated in history. Not long ago we celebrated the tercentenary of the Great Ejectment of 1662, when two thousand incumbents of the

Established Church in England were thrown out of their parishes because they refused to subscribe publicly to the unscriptural regulations of the Act of Uniformity. Parliament did not leave it at that, however, but passed a series of inhuman acts which made it illegal for the dissenters to assemble and worship God according to their own consciences; and these acts were enforced with the utmost severity. The years 1660 to 1688 saw one of the most disgraceful periods in English history, as Christian people persecuted Christian people with fanatical vengeance. You can read this revolting chronicle in such a book as Gerald Cragg's *Puritanism in the Period of the Great Persecution,*[2] where he tells how officers of the law broke into the homes and meetinghouses of dissenters, drove them out into the street, and there beat them with pikestaffs and musket butts, so that many victims died, while others were maimed for life. You can read how the dissenter was arrested and taken to the local tavern for humiliating trial before a sadistic judge; how the court levied a fine that might ruin him for life and, if he could not pay, seized his house, his furniture, his tools—everything that he owned. You can read how the dissenter might be sent to prison, or deported to a penal colony, or, if he were a man of influence, sentenced to death. Yet strangest of all, you can read a chapter which concludes with these words:

With humble amazement, the greatest spokesman of the persecuted groups noted that their sufferings had led to fuller life and to incalculable spiritual benefits. When the Lord had already

[2] (New York: Cambridge University Press, 1957).

spread a table before them in the presence of their enemies, they would gratefully rest in the conviction that goodness and mercy would follow them all the days of their lives.[3]

Still the pattern is being repeated. All over the world today there are churches under the cross, our Christian brethren in non-Christian environments who suffer persecution for righteousness' sake. They ask our prayers but not our sympathy, and certainly not our admiration. Far from resenting their trials, they rejoice in them, accepting them as a challenge to the Church, to the vitality of her faith, the authenticity of her hope, and the power of her love. Such a challenge, they declare, compels the Christian community to go the way of renewal. It forces the Church to be independent of the world, independent from worry over daily bread, independent from the danger of conceit, independent from every aspiration toward external power. It forces the Church to *be* the Church, to rely solely on God and on the Word of God, to stand or fall on nothing but the inherent power of the gospel.

Can you not see, then, why Jesus pointed to persecution as a pathway to happiness? He did not promise that we should enjoy being kicked around by the world, but he did promise that the wounds we suffer in the daily battle for righteousness become the one insignia which authenticates our membership in the greatest company that this world has ever known. "Rejoice, and be exceeding glad: . . . for so persecuted they the prophets which were before you."

[3] *Ibid.,* p. 87.

It is said of one of the early Christian martyrs that as the flames began to consume his flesh, his executioners snarled, "This is the end of you! What have you got to say now?" With the light of heaven on his face, the martyr replied through his agony, "I reckon that the sufferings of this present time are not worthy to be compared with the glory which shall be revealed in us."

That great saint had grasped not only the truth of the eighth beatitude but the crucially important truth which is common to all the Beatitudes. The teaching of Jesus from a mountaintop in Galilee, if we are going to make sense of it, must be set in the perspective of eternity. We must understand that when Jesus spoke of life he spoke of the whole of life, and not simply of that particular segment limited by the boundaries of what we call birth and death, or even limited by the boundaries of history. In the most complete sense the promises contained in some of the Beatitudes cannot be fulfilled in this world of time and space. Jesus did not intend that they should be fulfilled here; and to leave no doubt where the eighth beatitude is concerned, Jesus stated it explicitly—"Rejoice, and be exceeding glad: for great is your reward in heaven."

The book of Revelation is like a drama set on a two-level stage, the action taking place simultaneously on both levels. On the lower level is a scene of violence, bloodshed, and catastrophe, as though all the powers of hell have been unleashed to ravage the earth in wanton destruction; and in the midst of it, suffering excruciating agony, is the church of Jesus Christ. On the higher level is a scene of eternal bliss, as a great multitude assembles before the throne of God to sing his unending praise. Dressed in white robes, and with palm branches in their hands, are the martyrs who have suffered persecution for the Word of God and who now dwell in everlasting felicity. This, according to the inspired author of Revelation, is a picture of the whole of reality—a vivid, dramatic commentary on the promise of Jesus to his persecuted saints, "Rejoice, and be exceeding glad: for great is your reward in heaven."

The Beatitudes *have* to end with a warning about persecution, simply because the Beatitudes are in reality a self-portrait of Jesus. He incarnated all of them perfectly: he humbled himself, he was a man of sorrows, he was meek and lowly of heart, he was the righteousness of God, he showed compassion, he had no guile, he came as the Prince of Peace. And where did it take him? To a cross, to the ultimate persecution, as it takes there every man who, in a world that defies God, submits himself to the laws of God's kingdom. But Jesus rejoiced in his cross. The author of Hebrews writes of him, "Who for the joy that was set before him endured the cross, despising the shame, and is set down at the right hand of the throne of God" (12:2). Jesus rejoiced in the Cross because by faith he saw beyond the Crucifixion to the Resurrection, beyond the darkness of Good Friday to the brilliant light of Easter Day.

In that perspective alone we shall trust our Lord's promise and believe that if, for the sake of righteousness, we have to suffer any kind of persecution, it will ultimately be a pathway to happiness. In that perspective we shall trust every promise that Jesus made from the mountaintop in Galilee.

Because this is God's world, because God is all-powerful, and because God has all eternity in which to fulfill his purpose for our lives, therefore we shall submit ourselves to the laws of his kingdom, assured that they will lead to eternal blessedness.

God our Father, whose blessed Son didst walk the way of a cross, we entreat thee for thine obedient servants who have denied themselves and taken up their cross and followed Christ. We pray for thy Church, where its liberties have been crushed, its saints persecuted, and where men have borne witness, even to the shedding of their blood. Give them the courage to endure, and let them take unto themselves the whole armor of God, that they may be able to withstand in the evil day. Assure them that they are the lights of the world in their generation and that through them thou art sending out mighty influences that shall be for the healing of all men and for reconciliation among the nations. Grant that we also may take our share of hardship as good soldiers of Jesus Christ and may count it all joy to suffer for righteousness' sake. Beyond the darkness of every Calvary fix our hope on the brightness of Easter Day, that, sharing the fellowship of our Lord's sufferings, we may also share the power of his resurrection.

And now unto him that is able to do exceeding abundantly above all that we ask or think, according to the power that worketh in us, unto him be glory in the Church by Christ Jesus throughout all ages, world without end. Amen.